WITH COURAGE AND TRUST
20 Years with Police Dogs

by

David Brown

Scarthin Books

1994

Photograph Courtesy of the Nottingham Evening Post

Phototypesetting: Paragon Typesetters

Printing: Redwood Books

ISBN 0907 758 78 9

CONTENTS

Foreword   4
Introduction   5

PART I   MY CAREER WITH DOGS

Chapter 1   Early Days, From Pets To a Career   8
Chapter 2   Dogs At Work   14
Chapter 3   It Wasn't Alright On The Night   27

PART II   HISTORY OF THE POLICE DOG IN ENGLAND

Chapter 4   Mainly Bloodhounds   34
Chapter 5   The First Police Dogs In England   40
Chapter 6   Specialist Search Dogs   65
Chapter 7   Scent And Tracking   67
Chapter 8   Incredible But True – Tracking Stories   73
                       from South Africa

PART III   YOU AND YOUR DOG

Chapter 9   The Law Relating To You And Your Dog   76
Chapter 10   Your Dog, Your Choice   80
Chapter 11   The Care Of Your Dog   82
Chapter 12   Common Health Problems   90

PART IV   TRAINING YOUR DOG

Chapter 13   About Training   94
Chapter 14   The Training Exercises   100
Chapter 15   Novelty Tricks   113
Chapter 16   Common Behaviour Problems   115

PART V   APPENDICES   120

Dogs within the Nottinghamshire Police Forces before the
   inception of Dog Sections
Nottingham City Police Dog Section
Nottinghamshire Constabulary Police Dog Section
Police Dog National Champions

FOREWORD

Having known David Brown for many years I am very happy to write this foreword to his book.

The History of Police Dogs I found most interesting and am sure it will be enjoyed by dog lovers and the public in general; the chapters on training are simple to follow and are ample illustration of the author's expertise in different fields.

The chapters on health and behaviour problems are filled with good common sense as one would expect from a man who has spent his adult life looking after working dogs.

In all I found the book to be a very good read.

Percy Elliott
International Championship Dog Judge.
Author of "The Complete German Shepherd Dog".
Former chairman of the German Shepherd Dog League of Great Britain.

INTRODUCTION

The English are generally classed as a dog loving nation, yet there are those who are 'anti-dog', and who can blame them when they put forward the following in justification: dogs are a menace to society when they:
· Stray and wander about
· Pollute both by noise and excrement
· Spread disease
· Cause injury to people and other animals
· Cause road accidents

However, it has long been recognised that training the dog and educating the owner or handler will alleviate all the above. It is in the interests of the 'pro-dog' lobby to aim for responsible ownership so that everyone may come to appreciate the companionship and working ability of the dog. It is with this in mind that I have put pen to paper.

The police dog owes its very existence to those members of the public who, for whatever reason, donate their dog to the Service. The gift dog is still relied upon to fill the ranks and it is my hope that previous owners of these dogs may read this book and so to them I express a heartfelt 'Thank you'.

I would also like to make a dedication to my wife, Diane, who has suffered years of 'dogging' at my side, be it in rain, wind, hail or snow, at Trials, rooting in bookshops or woken up in the middle of the night with tales of 'dog heroism'. Also to son Shaun and daughter Alison who have been avid listeners to my doggy stories. I wish to make a final dedication to the often unsung heroes of the peace, the Police Dogs. Not always confined to detecting lawbreakers, they are used in many other roles including that of a deterrent and searching for both property and missing persons. They also now have a prominent position in the detection of Drugs and Explosives. My purpose is to reach the majority of dog owners who, for whatever reason, have been unable to obtain the guidance and training they need and those who have tried and given up.

I will highlight the dogs in my career of 20 years of Police Dog Handling and Training but I also wish to make a dedication to the other dogs who have been and still are part of my life, the family pets – mongrel Shandy, German Shepherds Sheba, Dell and Regan, Yorkshire Terrier Ben and Border Collie Flint.

When asked to describe a Police Dog, most people will simply describe the German Shepherd dog. The true answer is, 'any dog, of whatever description be it mongrel or pedigree, that assists the Police to carry out their duties.' The dog is, in fact, a tool, its natural abilities harnessed, honed and utilised for a particular purpose. It would be wrong, therefore, to choose just one particular breed. What has been chosen, throughout the evolution of the police dog, is the most suitable breed for the purpose at that time.

Today the German Shepherd is in vogue as the general purpose police dog, one of the main reasons being that the dog 'looks the part'. I could go further, describing the pros and cons of all breeds but even then there are exceptions to the rule. A Standard Poodle could perform equally as well as the best of the Shepherds but I am afraid the handler would be forever suffering taunts and having to prove his credibility, especially on a Friday night.

MY CAREER WITH DOGS

Initial Dog Training Course, September 1974, Epperstone Manor.

Such fidelity of dogs in protecting what is committed to their charge, such affectionate attachments to their masters, such jealousy of strangers, such incredible acuteness of nose in following a track, such keenness in hunting – what else do they evince but that these animals were created for the use of man?

CICERO (106 – 43 BC)

Chapter 1

EARLY DAYS
– FROM PETS TO A CAREER

Throughout my childhood and youth there had never been a dog in, near to or related to my home. I had never fussed, spoken to, or even taken a dog for a walk. Dogs were pavement foulers and things that chased pedal cycles, namely mine. Odds on, a slip to the ground on any patch of grass would always produce the undesirable smell and brown stain that would get me into trouble upon returning home. It is quite fair to say that I was not attracted to the species in any way.

The first time I took notice of any dog was as a 16-year-old youth. Together with friends, idling on a local recreation ground, we watched a Police Dog Handler put his dog through its paces. Sitting on a park bench we were enthralled by the precision heelwork, sendaway, distance control and other basic exercises. The handler, dressed in full uniform, was no doubt taking a break from foot patrol to practice in front of a less than critical audience. After 30 minutes or so, with a polite wink and a smile, he carried on his way. (Some years later, I identified him as PC 257 Dean with Police Dog Shadow). "When I have a dog, that's how I want it to be trained", was my own comment, echoed by the others. I never gave this remark any more thought until years later.

I joined the Nottinghamshire Constabulary, as a Police Cadet, aged 17 years, in September 1965 stationed at Headquarters Epperstone Manor. My only contact with Police Dogs was to deliver mail to the nearby compound. A 6-foot (2m) high fence surrounded the compound and kennel block, and no one was allowed to enter. A knock and a shout at the gate produced a growl, not from the dogs, but from the Sergeant in charge who'd been made to leave the warmth of his hut. It was to be some time before the Dog Section had

The kennels at headquarters, Epperstone Manor.

the luxury of a true building. Becoming a Regular member of the Force on 1st January 1967 I had no aspirations towards the Dog Section and was content to walk the beat.

During the early part of 1968 I acquired my first dog. A society reject, found wandering, I saved him from collection by the RSPCA and brought him home as a pet. He was a long-haired mongrel dog, with all the looks of a Border Collie, but light brown in colour. A stray of unknown origin and aged between 3 and 4 years, unkempt, neglected but truly artful in self-preservation, Shandy as I named him, showed no evidence of any previous training. He fought anything that moved and took off any time he felt like it, only to return in the evening for his dinner. I had no idea about dog training and there was no local dog training club where I could learn.

In 20 months service I had only previously encountered a Dog Handler as he passed by in his van, a comforting sight whilst walking the beat on 'nights'. (I might add, that in Force Orders a Police Officer was allowed to have his own dog accompany him at night, provided the dog met certain criteria and had been assessed by the officer in charge of the Dog Section. However, I knew of no fellow officer who had taken advantage of this).

It wasn't until August of that year, 1968, at 3am on a warm moonless Sunday morning, that I first experienced a

Police Dog in action. Working the night shift, with no communication other than the hourly contact point, it was by chance the Sub-Divisional Sergeant saw me walking and picked me up in his van. "We're going to a burglary", he said, as we were joined in convoy by a patrol car and dog van.

Arriving at an isolated clubhouse, we found a broken window and open door, the handler put his dog to work. The premises were quckly searched, with no trace of the offenders. Using harness and line, the dog was put to 'track' from the open door. Nose down, the dog set off, three of us following the handler, in indian file. Occasionally stumbling in the blackness, none dared use a torch, or speak for fear of provoking the handler's wrath by possibly giving our position away. We negotiated fields and pathways, and after what appeared to be an eternity, with all of us sweating and out of breath, the handler's torch came on. There, some 50 yeards ahead, I saw three youths. A challenge was shouted but they responded by running away into the blackness.

The Police Dog was released and by torchlight in the ensuing chase I saw the dog take hold of a leg being hastily pulled through the gap in a fence. The dog detained this youth until the arrival of the handler, and was then sent in pursuit of a second felon who had climbed the fence and was still running away. A distant scream, and a thud denoted once again the dog had completed his task. With two now in custody, the dog was put to search for the third. A short time later the dog began barking and our last quarry was found lying in a large puddle.

The youths later admitted this and numerous other crimes which, no doubt, could quite easily have remained unsolved but for the expertise of the Police Dog, Mountbrowne Wotan, an 8-year old dog, handled by PC 260 Rebaudi.

As with all good stories, this Police Dog grew bigger and blacker in colour, with every telling. Once more I said to myself, "That's how I want my dog to be trained".

The ambition to train a dog properly was now kindled but I was frustrated as to where to find this instruction. Shandy continued his ways until he grew so out of control I was embarrassed at my failure. Luckily, an elderly man hearing of my plight, and needing a companion himself, offered a further home. The adoption completed, I soon saw the fruits of his new owner's knowledge and skill; Shandy was quickly brought under control. Food must have played a great part, as he soon grew too fat for some of life's adventures and settled down to grow old gracefully.

I decided to start from the beginning and buy a puppy. In the latter part of 1968 I purchased Sheba, an 8-week old German Shepherd bitch. A pedigree, I was assured, although there were no papers to be had. Again, with no help or direction, 'training' was left to my own devices.

I moved house and some two years later, I eventually located a dog training club. Sheba was, in my opinion, now trained and well-behaved. What a shock! At our first attendance she became totally out of control in the presence of other dogs. She was aggressive and, with my apparent lack of control, became a total distraction to the class. Perfectly behaved at home, there was a complete character change when she went to class. The simplest exercises were difficult and my confidence quickly disappeared. Problem dogs and their handlers were not catered for at the club and were immediately made to feel social outcasts. With no real help, and having to sit out most of the time, I soon gave up these classes. Thus the many reasons for enrolling were, in fact, working against me. Sheba was a good companion and housedog and I consoled myself with that for a time.

"Let her have some pups, that'll slow her down", I was told and for this, the wrong reason, I embarked on dog breeding. Having approached a fellow 'club reject' who owned a nice-looking German Shepherd dog, we agreed that a mating should take place the next time Sheba came into season. With naivety in its extreme, Sheba was introduced to the other dog by putting them together in an outside garage. Looking through a window, all the dogs would do was play together. Thinking they were too shy with an audience we decided to leave them alone for an hour. Later I took Sheba home, fully expecting a pregnancy to follow.

There was no result from this liaison, and after making a few enquiries I was pointed in the direction of a local breeder who offered the services of a stud dog for a fee of £25.00. Naive again, with no knowledge of genetics and dog selection and no advice given, I chose the stud dog purely upon my own interpretation of good looks.

Sheba subsequently gave birth to 11 pups in the summer of 1971. During the following six weeks, eight of these puppies died from what was diagnosed as 'Fading Puppy Syndrome'. Two of the remaining pups were sold at 9 weeks of age, without pedigree although quite obviously German Shepherds. With the last puppy, a bitch named Dell, I fell in the trap of keeping her as company for Sheba, thus giving me another dog to train.

Becoming a mother did nothing for Sheba, her temperament remained unaltered and, if anything, made her more aggressively protective. I again looked for a dog training club and found one specialising in German Shepherds. Sheba, I was told, was now beyond redemption but Dell, being a puppy, was enrolled. A very shy and somewhat nervous individual, Dell was growing up under the shadow and influence of her mother, therefore instinctively playing second fiddle. Naivety, once more, prevented me from realising this and therefore Dell's spirit was continually being quelled. By the time this was pointed out to me, her temperament had developed to a degree that she would do nothing of her own volition and she was quite shallow in character.

The mistakes I made are common amongst novice owners. I now had two dogs with whom my ambitions of attaining a high standard in training would never be realised. What do you do under these circumstances? Wait possibly another ten years to start again? Find homes for these dogs and start afresh? No-one can give the appropriate advice, it becomes your decision. Sheba, now a mature dog was to stay. Dell was readily offered another home within the family.

Once more I decided to start with a puppy. From friends I had by now made within the dog world, I was given sound advice. This time I was going to a reputable breeder, to select a German Shepherd pup, from sound pedigree stock with a good working temperament.

In August 1973 I purchased a 9-week old dog pup and gave him the name Rudi. On the day of his collection from the breeder I took great care making him comfortable, wrapping him in blankets and settling him down on the back seat of the car. Within minutes of starting the journey home he negotiated the distance between us, climbed onto my lap and was then calmly sick all over me. Such an intimate introduction!

As Rudi came of age, at 6 months, I enrolled at a number of dog training clubs, educating myself in the knowledge and techniques available. I quickly became interested in Working Trials and there came into direct contact with Police Dog Handlers and their dogs. As a result I made application to join the Police Dog Section, taking Rudi with me if we were both found suitable.

On the 2nd September 1974 we were both accepted for training. Rights of ownership of Rudi were transferred to the Chief Constable and a 13-week Initial Training Course lay ahead of us. I quickly realised it was me, the handler, who

With Rudi after completing the Initial Training Course

needed training more than the dog, both physically and mentally. I was unfit and awkward in handling techniques. I was being taught the true art of handling a dog, an intelligent animal, using him as an extension to my own senses. A progressive programme ensured that with the end of course test successfully completed we were ready for the streets, or so I thought! We had only passed the first test, learning is never complete or any situation the same, either for dog or handler. We had only just begun to know each other. Habits, a flick of the finger, a nod of the head, a look, lift of the nose, prick of the ears, all part of our language, a team, each complementing the other. To search, locate and retrieve, indicate the presence of, to track, to hunt and to chase, to have the most intelligent quarry of all – MAN.

Chapter 2

DOGS AT WORK

There have been countless incidents throughout my service as an Operational Police Dog Handler. The personal incidents which follow, progressing from my earliest days with Rudi, up to the present, portray the different abilities and use of the Police Dog.

Prisoners From Nowhere
At 2am, on a foggy winter night, Coal Board Security reported that numerous vehicles had been broken into on a colliery car park and property stolen. At 4.30am I arrived with Rudi, an afterthought request causing the delay, and made a search for the person/s responsible. About ¼ mile away I found an open-top sports car, parked and unattended. While I made a check of it I allowed Rudi to run free and stretch his legs, no longer under command to search. He normally never wandered more than a few yards away from me, and I soon became aware that he was missing. Whistles and calling did not bring him back but resulted in muffled barks from a nearby copse. Running towards the trees, which were in complete darkness, I was suddenly confronted by two motionless figures, in dark clothing and wearing crash helmets. The dog was circling, ensuring that neither moved; thankfully, as it turned out, for when searched, both men were in possession of a half scissor which they had used for breaking into the cars, but equally could have been used as weapons aginst me.

A Quick Result
One night a burglary occurred at a licensed club, in the centre of a housing estate, and two men were seen to run away. Travelling 25 miles in as many minutes to the scene I was told that a full search of the area had been made by a number of section officers with no result, but it was believed the men

14

Rudi competing in the No. 4 (Eastern) Region Police Dog Trials.

were still in the vicinity. The search area consisted of some 40 houses and gardens. Within two minutes of being put to search, Rudi found both men hiding deep within nearby blackberry bushes.

In September 1979 I went to Rudi's kennel, ready for the night shift, and found him lying dead. During the day he had shown no signs or symptoms of illness and his death came as a complete shock. A post-mortem revealed that he had died from Canine Parvo-virus, a disease which had only just surfaced and was spreading in epidemic proportions throughout the country. Rudi was one of the first fatal cases in the area and at that time no vaccine had been produced.

We had learned a lot together and it was a traumatic end to our partnership.

A volunteer now had to be found, a replacement Police Dog. Such a dog was Blue, brought into the Police Station on more than one occasion as a stray. The owner eventually made it permanent by donating him to the Dog Section. There was a dog of the same name already in service and many hours were spent choosing an alternative name. Ryan was finally chosen as the name for this 18-month old

German Shepherd dog, who from the very start indicated his dislike of the training field.

The Initial Course started on 7th January 1980 and for the first three weeks Ryan went everywhere with a long line attached to him, in order that he could easily be caught whenever he took the opportunity to wander. It was quite apparent that he had been used to doing exactly as he pleased. However, introducing him to tracking, was like taking a duck to water, and it became Ryan's greatest pleasure, sometimes to my annoyance. Whilst performing other exercises his attention would suddenly divert and nose to the ground, off he would go, oblivious to my calls.

Oh S**t

For both novice and experienced handlers, one of the jobs of the Initial Course was to clean the kennels first thing in the morning. This entailed hosing down any excrement etc. into the drainage gulleys which, in turn, emptied into a sump drain and then into a cesspit. To keep the amount of effluent down and to save blockages, the sump was fitted with a colander type bucket. These buckets were emptied by hand, with a hooked rod which held the bucket handle. After a minute or so to allow the bucket to drain, the bucket was rather gingerly carried, at arms length, out of the kennel block, balanced, whilst climbing over a fence, and then tipped onto a nettle bed.

My turn came, and having done it many times before, I decided on a short cut. Leaning over the fence I gave the rod and bucket a swing, intending for the bucket to empty on the slightly upward arc. That upward arc suddenly became over-exaggerated and the next thing I saw was the bucket heading back towards me. As in a dream, my legs couldn't move fast enough and before I could do anything more I was covered from head to foot by the contents. It took me one full day of showering to get rid of the smell but a lot longer to get rid of the comments!

With the course completed Ryan soon showed his expertise in the art of tracking.

A Light At Night

At 2.30am a patrolling officer spotted two lamps being used across fields in a rural area frequented by poachers. These lamps were extinguished when the Police vehicle was apparently seen. Their exact position and subsequent movement was lost in the darkness.

Arriving 30 minutes later I put Ryan to track, close to the initial sighting. It was clear that poachers had been in action and that dogs were being used. Ryan began following the scent, through fields onto a main 'A' class road, along that road and onto further fields. Negotiating all manner of terrain, from ploughed field to grass, crossing ditches, hedgerows, fences and barbed wire we continued. I believed, and subsequently found out, that the poachers knew we were in pursuit, the villains had spotted us on the skyline some distance behind them. The track, in part, followed a railway line and visual indications such as footprints and scuffmarks were evident in the frost beginning to form on the wooden sleepers. Using a radio, I was able to position other Police Officers ahead of me and eventually, on the perimeter of a racecourse, a man and dog were detained.

I was three minutes behind as I allowed Ryan to continue and track through this point, onwards in pursuit of a second man and dog. A short time later, approaching a wooded area, I could hear someone crashing through the undergrowth. I shouted a challenge at which came the response, "Lets call it a day. I bet you're as knackered as me." A few moments passed before a man and his Lurcher bitch emerged from the wood. The total distance of this track was some 4½ miles and whilst returning with the man, who was under arrest for 'night poaching', the dogs played together as we talked of dog matters. Both of us operating dogs in a different manner, each getting our own pleasure and reward, even if one was outside the law.

Football At Night
During the early hours a vehicle was found on land frequented by poachers. The land belonging to a wealthy estate, was overseen by gamekeepers with an electronic alarm system. The system had been triggered in the vicinity of the vehicle and as I was making a search of the area, in the company of a gamekeeper, two men came jogging towards us, from nearby woodland. Jumping and 'heading' the air, as if playing football, their reply to my questions was, "We're just football training, youth", and would admit to nothing else. On the harness Ryan back-tracked from the men into the woodland and after a few yards, indicated a number of freshly killed rabbits, all strung together and concealed in the undergrowth.

The dog continued tracking, eventually to a rabbit warren, and then made to return. With the two men having been left in the company of other officers, the gamekeeper had accompanied me and neither he nor I could detect how the rabbits had been caught. Suspecting the use of nets we returned to the dead rabbits and I put the dog to search for such articles. Ryan disappeared into the darkness, not to re-appear for some 20 minutes. Suspecting that he had been on his own tracking expedition, I harnessed him up again and effectively asked him to take me where I believed he had already been. The dog tracked for 1/3 mile then stopped and indicated a man who was hiding amongst the ferns clutching his whippet dog. All three men subsequently admitted poaching and using the dog to catch the rabbits.

Burglars Two

At 11pm, one summer evening, a shop was broken into and at the point of entry a large amount of blood was found. A quantity of cigarettes and other goods had been stolen and two men seen to run away. Whilst making a search of the area, at 11.30pm, a report was received that two men, one with his leg covered in blood, had been given a lift to a near-by village; carrying goods similar to those stolen, they were last seen on the main street. At 11.45pm, together with other officers, I made a search of the area but found nothing. Numerous people were about and it would have been impossible for the dog to identify a particular track.

As the other officers left I remained, with Ryan, keeping in the shadows of the now empty streets. Some time later I saw two men at the rear of a row of terraced houses. They were walking on tiptoe carrying their shoes. Creeping along, they looked every bit the comic book burglars. Both turned at my shouted challenge, and upon seeing the dog stood still. One had severe lacerations to his right foot but neither admitted any knowledge of the burglary, or had any property on them. Ten minutes later, with the men safely in custody under suspicion, I put Ryan to back-track. From the point I had first seen the men he tracked along streets and through allotment gardens, eventually to a garden shed. Opening the door I was confronted by a small Aladdin's Cave. Both men later admitted this offence, and numerous others.

A Courting Couple, Indeed!

Called to a large vehicle compound one night, I found a strong smell of petrol everywhere. Two people had been seen inside the pound and although vehicles had been broken into and petrol caps removed, neither the offenders nor anything else could be found. As I made a search with Ryan, he located a small hole in the perimeter wire fence, and a short distance from this he found a number of plastic drums full of petrol. These drums had been hidden and it was decided to keep watch, using other officers.

Some time later, whilst I was dealing with other matters, a vehicle came to the scene and the occupants made to recover the drums. Somehow they were disturbed, they discovered the police presence, and made a getaway in their vehicle. The registration number was noted but it was recorded as having 'no current keeper'. Making a mobile search of the area I discovered the vehicle, apparently abandoned, on a wooded lane a ½-mile away. Putting Ryan to track, he had covered less than 50 yards when he indicated a man and woman lying under a hedgerow. Both denied any knowledge of the vehicle or the theft of petrol. They were arrested and taken to the Police Station where their excuse for being under the hedgerow was that they had been overcome by passion and were taking advantage of the seclusion.

Returning to the exact spot where the couple had been found I put Ryan to search. From beneath the flattened undergrowth, hidden from view, the dog recovered a bunch of keys, containing both the keys to the car and the house keys of the man in custody. Presented with this evidence both admitted offences of theft.

As Ryan approached 8 years of age, he was to be retired due to ill health and a new dog trained. As though he had heard the news, Ryan was to end his career almost as it began.

Circumstantial Climax
At 3.45am a vehicle being chased through Forestry Commission land by a patrol car, was abandoned, the offenders making their escape into thick woodland.

Arriving with Ryan a few minutes later, the dog began to track, from the open drivers' door. Crossing woodland, open ground, a railway line and footbridges, the track continued for 5 miles, taking 1 hour 20 minutes. From directions given by me, with the use of radio, three men were intercepted a ½-mile ahead. They were arrested and taken away as Ryan continued tracking eventually to the exact point of interception. With this evidence, after initial denials, the men admitted taking the vehicle and using it in the course of a burglary.

With the impending course only 6 weeks away, there was an

acute shortage of dogs acceptable for training. Any dog offered was brought to the kennels to be thoroughly assessed. One such dog was a 13-month old German Shepherd. Emaciated and looking more like a greyhound, he had been rescued from a life tied to a dustbin in someone's backyard. Cowering and snarling at the back of the kennel he looked set to be rejected for future training, if only on temperament alone. However, with no other dog to choose from, I took a closer look. Examining his somewhat visible skeleton I could see that there was no deformity and, with a good covering of flesh and muscle, he would have the build for a fine working dog. Although he was too large to conform to current breed standards, in most respects and had a height of 28in (71cm) at the shoulder, he would still look the part.

I decided to give him a chance and spent days winning him over, with food playing a great part. His temperament steadily changed towards me, although not to anyone else – he was highly aggressive and had no trust. He was given the name Laser and taken home and introduced to my family. Even though I was feeding him with up to six meals daily and he steadily gained weight, I dared not take him out straight away for fear of being accused of neglect.

Laser soon adapted to his new home and his first trick was to take washing from the line as quickly as it was pegged out. Next, during the night, he broke out from his kennel, through the wire mesh to toilet on the lawn and then raid the dustbin. After a further occurrence later the same week, I had to replace the wire with welded mesh. Laser needed no training in cleanliness! Six weeks later, my patience was rewarded, Laser became outwardly acceptable for the Initial Training course.

Ryan was retired but continued to have part-time work, under the control of my son, Shaun. Being a perfectly behaved pet dog with his 12-year old handler, he performed well at dog club obedience classes. Shaun always took great pains to state, to whoever complimented him, that all credits for Ryan's good behaviour were his. This was the truth, he re-handled an experienced working dog who knew how to play up if he wished.

Once the Initial Course had started on 1st September 1986, I was to find problems with Laser that I had not anticipated. In all discipline exercises I had a battle to win his confidence. A constant uphill struggle was evident when it became clear that Laser preferred 'flight' rather than 'fight' whenever he felt stress. Whenever he was confronted by

Growing up with dogs: Shaun in 1978 aged 5 with Regan (left) and Rudi; aged 12 with Ryan, and with me and Laser in 1992.

something he could not understand he would run away from it. Tracking, searching and criminal work were done with enthusiasm, but it was heelwork that first exposed this problem within him. I could think of no cause for this behaviour, unless it possibly stemmed from his previous owners' attempts at training. The command 'heel' whilst off the lead, was enough for him to show the whites of his eyes and run. However, with patience and understanding, this was gradually overcome and the course completed on time.

Within two months Laser was to take over where Ryan had left off. Once again I had a Police Dog with tracking expertise.

Hit Him And Run
At 12.55am, on a February night, a Traffic Patrol Officer was beaten unconscious by one of four men he had questioned after stopping their vehicle, in a remote rural area of a main 'A'-class road. The men had made off, leaving the vehicle and disappeared into the night. Some 20 minutes later I arrived at the scene with Laser, who took no time in locating a track into nearby woodland. Exiting onto roads and through fields we eventually came back to within 200 yards of the scene, a circular route of about 1½ miles. It was there Laser indicated a man hiding in a hedge bottom. This man subsequently proved to be the one guilty of the assault.

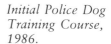

Initial Police Dog Training Course, 1986.

22

Self Service But Not When Closed!

A year later, almost to the day, I attended a burglary at a self service petrol station. At 11.35pm two men had been disturbed inside the premises and made their escape across adjacent fields. Arriving at midnight I put Laser to track, from the point of last sighting. He followed a route crossing fields and pushing through hawthorn hedgerows. While crossing a ploughed field, the dog suddenly dropped and there, between his front feet, was a pink rubber household glove. Recovered as evidence, the glove also proved we were still on track. After 30 minutes we were still in the fields when I knew, by the dog's manner, we were closing on our quarry. The pace quickened and Laser's head came up, into the wind. Turning onto another field I saw, 150 yards ahead of me, two men crouching and running under cover of the hedgerow. I shouted a challenge, at which both turned and on seeing the dog about to be released, stood still in the classic 'hands raised' position. I found both to be in possession of housebreaking implements and they readily admitted the burglary. A few months later, one of these men was involved in the murder of a shopkeeper in another county. I wonder if a different tale might have been told of that night, had I not had my dog to confront them.

A Rubbish Place To Hide

At 12.05am on an August night a youth had been disturbed trying to steal a motor car and was chased into a large housing estate and lost from sight. Other Police Officers spotted the youth on numerous occasions as they searched, but were unable to locate him. Attending the scene, I made a systematic search of the area, including all back gardens and outhouses. After some 45 minutes of searching Laser jumped up and sniffed at the lid of a household wheelie bin and then gave a deep growl. I knew I'd found my man — lifting the lid I saw a well-built youth of 17 years sitting with his knees under his chin.

Mr Houdini, I Presume!

At 3.15pm, on a sunny afternoon, I arrived at a derelict factory complex where two men had already been arrested for theft of lead from the roof. A third man was believed hiding in the vicinity. With Laser a full search of the buildings was made but we found nothing. The roof area was dangerous to walk on so I summoned the assistance of the Fire Brigade. With a ride in 'Simon Snorkel', the hydraulic lift, a full scan

Why not follow our lead?

Openings for dogs in force

IT'S far from being a dog's life in the Notts police force, judging by the contended look of its four-legged recruits.

And there are openings for young whipper-snappers to join at the moment, as the Notts force is at least four animals below strength.

There is a nationwide shortage of German Shepherd dogs being donated to the police by members of the public.

The Notts section has 28 operational German Shepherd dogs, and ten English springer spaniels used as specialist search dogs.

The dogs trained at Notts Police Head-quarters have to be between 11 months and two and half years old and are normally donated by the public.

After a 13-week training course, each dog lives at the home of a policeman.

POSTPHOTO 93118/19
● Police dog Laser, under the guidance of PC Dave Brown, has won his cap after making a number of arrests

POSTPHOTO 93118A.4
● Laser is put through his paces by PC Dave Brown. INSET: The latest recruit, Buster

search was made of the roof but again there was nothing. As a result the Fire Brigade and all the other police officers left the scene. However, I was still suspicious that the third man was there, so I secreted myself and the dog in a corner of the main factory floor and decided to play a waiting game. Sure enough, 40 minutes later, the third man suddenly appeared at the farthest point away from me, diagonally across the floor. I don't know who was the most surprised, but he made the first jump. Like a squirrel up a tree, he shinned the wall next to him, heading for a hole in the roof above. Laser was sent to detain him but failed to make contact before he was through the hole and out onto the fragile asbestos roof.

Once more the Fire Brigade arrived, but with the same result. Our man had disappeared into thin air. This time a big show was made of leaving the area, including someone driving my van away and sounding the two-tone horns for good measure. I played another waiting game, in another part of the factory, beneath a hole in the roof I calculated to be in the direction of where the man had disappeared.

It was 5.20pm when I heard a movement above me. Keep-

Publicity for the Dog Section in the local paper, the Nottingham Evening Post.

ing in the shadows I saw two feet appear through the hole, then the rest of the body, emerging slowly and silently. Laser with his ears pricked gave a fixed stare. The man continued lowering himself, face to the wall. I took a pace forward with Laser on the leash and as our man touched the floor so did the dog's nose touch his backside. With a gambit of, "Do I need to get him to open his mouth", the man froze.

Final Score 3-1
With three thriving football clubs in Nottinghamshire, matchday was a headache, not only in respect of policing the crowds but also safeguarding their vehicles from thieves.

In an effort to combat this menace, many hours were spent patrolling and keeping the vehicles under observation. During one such day, at 7.50pm on a February evening, I and another officer were secreted, in positions overlooking an isolated lane full of private cars. With dogs at our side we were ready to pounce. At 8.30pm, four youths aged 17 and 18 appeared, one riding a pedal cycle and acting as a lookout. They made a full inspection of each car, discussing which to break into, as they went along. They then left the lane, returning 15 minutes later, again peering through windscreens. Stopping at one particular vehicle, they crowded around it and it was then I heard the sound of breaking glass. A radio call alerted other dog patrols in the vicinity, together with my partner who emerged some 50 yards away from them. I was in no position to make a direct challenge but as the other officer did so, they all ran towards nearby waste ground and the blackness of the night. From the other end of the lane came two dog patrol vehicles. Blue lights shone as challenges were shouted and figures ran.

I recollect seeing one dog take a fleeing arm in the distance, highlighted under a street lamp. Last out onto the roadway, I crossed onto the waste ground, when, crashing towards me I saw my partner's dog. There was only me in his path and I commanded him back to his handler. As the dog turned and ran back into the blackness a furtive figure emerged from a hedgerow and began running towards me. As he looked up, an expression of horror came over his face and he turned quickly and made back through the hedgerow. Laser was sent to detain him, which he did, dragging him back through the hedge by the arm. Taking this prisoner out onto the road and handing him over to other officers, my partner and I decided to make a further search in the vicinity, as it transpired the other dog was in full pursuit when I had

Tom and Jerry.

inadvertently called him off, however, he had escaped.

On Tuesday, 2nd June 1992, a new dog entered my life. A liver-and-white English Springer Spaniel dog, aged 12 weeks. Two puppies were purchased together by the police, this one was called Jerry the other called Tom.

Awakened regularly at 1.30am, 4.30am and 6.30am, by the squeaking and howling of this distraught little hooligan, it wasn't until the 16th June that I could sleep until 6.30am without disturbance.

Jerry was eventually to be trained as a Specialist Search Dog and all his puppyhood was geared to this. However I quickly found out how the breed came by the name 'Springer'. I have never known a dog so agile or active. Anything within the boundary of a leap became part of the game. I had to be very careful, and still am to this day, where I put anything to prevent it becoming a playtoy. Jerry is a true character, he was easy to train and qualified in his new vocation on 26th February 1993.

Laser was by now looking old and his back legs getting weaker. Muscle wastage was evident and the Vet diagnosed bowel problems, probably cancer. His working days were now over. At 9.10am, on Wednesday, 30th March 1993, I held Laser as he was painlessly put to sleep.

Chapter 3

IT WASN'T ALRIGHT ON
THE NIGHT

The person who said, "It'll be all right on the night", has never trained or handled dogs. Here are a few of the 'out-takes' from the early days with each dog.

Away Supporters

Coming out of the Police Station, one night, I was confronted by a man who was quite breathless. "If you get there quick, you'll catch em", he said, as he hurriedly gave me more information. He had seen four youths break into the offices of a nearby football ground and emerge with crates of bottled beer, cigarettes etc. They were, at that moment, dividing their spoils on waste ground not far away.

Running to the scene, with dog on lead, I saw all that had been described. Creeping towards them I was spotted. I yelled a challenge for all to stand still or my Police Dog would be sent; at which, all four ran together. With at least 100 yards between us my dog was sent in pursuit, all his training brought into action. The dog quickly made up the ground, but then became confused. Four persons, side by side, "What do I do now?", he no doubt thought. The answer came quickly as they rounded a corner, out of my sight. I was running behind, giving all the verbal encouragement I could, and as I neared the corner, the dog came running back to me. With an expression and gait to match, he appeared to be saying, "Well that's an excellent job done, I've chased them away. What next?".

Luckily the youths were apprehended by other officers, not far away, by that time being too out of breath to run any further.

The Height of Fright

Searching a derelict building, I had sent the dog on ahead inside, whilst I stayed outside with another officer. After two or three minutes, hearing no sound from within, I recalled my dog. A frightening apparition, a large dark shape came flying at us from above. With a startled scream both of us turned to run as the shape hit the ground beside us. It was my dog, he had leapt out of a bedroom window, heedless of danger, on hearing my call. No injury was caused, but this was a salutary lesson, and never again would I be so careless.

Water Spaniel

Searching the banks of the River Trent, looking for a wanted person, my dog wind-scented another police officer on the opposite bank. Thinking it was our quarry, the dog ran and dived into the fast flowing waters intent on pursuit. Recalling the dog, it took twenty minutes and a run of one mile down-river before the dog clambered out tired and bedraggled. The search had to be started all over again, but this time the dog had learned his lesson.

Right Time, Right Place, Wrong Result

After a high speed chase along the M1 two youths abandoned a stolen vehicle and made off, on foot, over near-by fields with Traffic Officers in hot pursuit. However, these youths made good their escape. Making a search of the area I saw both youths in a field a short distance away. After being challenged both started to run towards woodland. My dog was sent to detain them, but after only a few yards a Dobermann dog came from nowhere at the speed of a missile and a dog fight ensued. The owner of this dog was too far away to be of any use and some time elapsed before the dogs could be truly separated. By this time the culprits were long gone.

Continuing with the search, I again spotted the youths in another field where I thought they could be easily reached. Once more challenged, to no avail, the youths ran and the dog was sent only to stop suddenly, as if hit by a brick wall. On reaching him I saw the cause, a wide canal, no doubt the dog thought, "I've tried this one before!", and I was quite thankful as I didn't relish the thought of wading or swimming across it either. Negotiating the canal via a bridge, the search was continued. Whilst walking along an old railway cutting a call came over the radio, "They're just in front of you", at which I caught movement ahead. Once more the dog was sent, but as he was half way another call came to the effect: 'not the ones the dog is after but those two looking up at you from the ditch, about 20 yards to the right'. Luckily I managed to recall the dog, just in time, and the youths were detained by other officers who were close by.

A Sweet Surprise
Attending a town centre burglary I found the premises surrounded, with a report that noises had been heard from inside. Numerous challenges had been shouted for the person|s inside to come out or show themselves, but there was no reply. I too, issued a challenge and warned that a Police Dog would be put in. No reply was forthcoming, and the dog was put in to search, with me remaining at the door. Minutes had elapsed without result so torch in hand, I decided to enter the building carefully and slowly go forward. Calling my dog and getting no response, I eventually reached the last room. On entering it I was greeted by the words, "Its about time you got here, the dog's mugged me for all the sweets in my pocket, I've only got me fags left".

Who's Afraid of the Bogyman?
At about 3am, on a May morning I had left the Dog Patrol van secluded and was walking through allotment gardens in the hope of catching thieves who had been breaking into gardeners' sheds. Suddenly the dog froze, his nose lifted with ears pricked. Looking between his ears and following the line of his nose I saw, in the distance, the figure of a man about three gardens away and close to one of the sheds. This was the first real job of the week and my adrenalin started to flow. The dog also sensed this and I heard a deep throated growl. At my shouted challenge, the man appeared to move. I thought, 'I'm not going to let this one get away' and sent the dog in full pursuit. I saw the dog leap and take the man, with all four feet off the floor, and they both collapsed in a heap. Running to them I could hear the dog growling, combined with the ripping of cloth. 'My God, he's fighting the dog', was my thought as I began shouting for the man to stop resisting. As I reached the heap on the floor I could see that my man had been nothing more than a well-dressed scarecrow. Shamefaced, I beat a hasty retreat back to the van, unable to do anything other than leave everything as it was.

The next day, while off duty, I went back to the allotments with thoughts of doing some explaining, when I was approached by an irate gardener, his first words being: "It's a pity you and your dog weren't around here last night". He then went on to relate how he had spent the whole of the previous day making and dressing up a scarecrow that, from a distance, would fool not only the birds but any human.

Vandals had wrecked it beyond repair and they must have had a dog with them because of all the pawprints on the seed bed. Thankfully they had not touched his shed and all his tools were safe. I left him with the promise that I would do everything in my power to catch the culprits.

A True Blue

Rudi was a dog that never did settle when travelling at high speed with blue light and two-tone horns. The moment the blue light was switched on and he heard the whirring sound, he immediately attacked the wiring loom suspended from the roof of the van. Although I tried to get to most places without the blue light, to save a defect report, I sometimes forgot and when I did so he never failed.

One night I returned home to collect Rudi, but whilst seeing to other things I was called away on an urgent matter. Rushing out and diving into the van I set off, blue light revolving and horns blowing. After a mile down the road I couldn't understand why the lamp was still working. It was then I realised I'd left the dog behind. Returning home, I found my wife standing at the gate, dog on leash. Putting him in the van I again roared off, everything blaring.

As I continued along, I could see from reflections that the light was still working. 'Great', I thought, 'after all this time, he's finally learned, what a good dog!' Upon reaching my destination I went to the back of the van, only to find the door swinging open and the dog almost breathless. No wonder he had not attacked the wiring loom, he'd been bracing himself on the floor of the van, hanging on for grim death to save himself from being flung out.

Now Who's in Trouble for Getting Dirty?

My son, Shaun, whilst serving as a Special Constable occasionally had the opportunity to 'double crew' with me on operational patrols. It was quite an unusual situation and once produced an incident to remember.

After a prolonged car chase, involving a stolen vehicle, there was an accident and three thieves made their escape, young legs quickly outstripping the older Traffic Officers. Getting to the scene within minutes, I took on direct pursuit, with the dog and tracking line, Shaun keeping to the tarmac and paths. Whilst he was in a position to 'head off' and relay messages and I was in the fields, he could also keep his uniform clean and not tarnish the image! Laser finally tracked to a muddy steam and I was wading along it, knee deep, with the dog, when Shaun appeared on the bank with a youth, saying with a broad grin, "Is this who you're looking for?"

As I had made my way along the stream he had been searching the adjacent gardens and found the youth secreted behind a garage. Taking his prisoner to a waiting patrol car, the driver asked where he had been found. Shaun started to reply, mentioning the 'dog man', when the driver interrupted saying, "That's not a dog man lad, it's your Dad, but don't let him get in my car in that state". With a hearty laugh he drove them to the Police Station leaving me to 'drip' my way back to the van.

What's in a Name

A specialist role has taken me into places where the presence of dogs is normally prohibited and given me some quite memorable moments. At a Remembrance Service inside a large and splendid building were gathered members of the RAF, together with ex-servicemen and the British Legion, with their flags and commemorative regalia.

Whilst working my dog I became aware of heads turning with furrowed brows. The dog was well-behaved, under control and working well when I realised it wasn't the dog, but my calls to him: "Jerry, Jerry", "Come on out of there Jerry"; the sounds of old forgotten war cries were echoing around the aisles.

Modern Art?

What could have been a most embarrasing moment was caused when Jerry answered the call of nature. No matter how we try to avoid it, an accident will sometimes happen. Once again, we were engaged on a search, in quite a prestigious building, thankfully with a stone floor. Jerry ran ahead of me around a corner. I immediately called him back to me and as we rounded the corner together I saw it: like the leaning tower of Pisa, a steaming obelisk confronted me. Jerry looked at it with an expression of, "Who on earth has done that!"

Hearing voices and footsteps closing down on me I had to act quickly, using a thin plastic glove produced from my

With Police Dog Jerry.

trouser pocket I quickly picked up the offending object, turned the glove inside out, and replaced it back in my pocket just as some officials appeared. There was no mark on the floor but there was an unmistakeable smell. Jerry sat quite angelically whilst we had a polite conversation, terminated quickly, with a mention of the state of the drains but without showing any of the eagerness I felt to cool my warm thigh.

Part II

HISTORY OF THE BRITISH POLICE DOG

The first police dogs on patrol in Nottingham city centre, May 1955, PC Curtis (left) and PC Walmsley.

With eye upraised, his masters' looks to scan, The joy, the solace, and the aid of man; The rich mans' guardian, the poor mans' friend, The only being faithful to the end.

GEORGE CRABBE (1754 – 1832)

Chapter 4

MAINLY BLOODHOUNDS

Before the establishment of Police Forces in the 19th century, the bloodhound assisted in the arrest of criminals, actively tracking the wrong-doer and leading the 'hue and cry'. Dr Johannes Caius, in his book, *Englishe Dogges* (printed 1576) well describes the bloodhound and its training:

> "These hounds, when they are to follow such fellows
> as we have before rehearsed, use not that liberty to
> range at will which they have otherwise when they are
> on game, when such purloiners make speedy way in
> flight, and being restrained and drawn backward from
> running at random, with the leash, the end whereof
> the owner holding in his hand, is led, guided, and
> directed, with such swiftness and slowness (whether he
> go on foot or whether he ride on horseback) as he
> himself in heart would wish, for the more easy
> apprehension of these venturous varlets."

The border area between England and Scotland was infested by robbers and marauders and in the 1700s a tax was levied on the local inhabitants for the upkeep of bloodhounds. A law in Scotland even dictated that whosoever denied entrance to one of these dogs would be treated as an accessory to the crime.

Generations before Sir Robert Peel there existed, especially in rural districts, 'Associations for the Prosecution of Felons' under whose authority bloodhounds were procured and trained principally for the purpose of tracking sheep stealers and other evil-doers.

A graphic description of the Bloodhound's ability is given in *The Chase* by William Somerville (1675 – 1742): –

> Soon the sagacious brute, his curling tail
> Flourished in air, low bending, plies around
> His busy nose, the steaming vapour snuffs

34

"The bloodhounds on the track", an etching taken from 'Cassell's Illustrated Family Paper', 14th June 1856.

Inquisitive, nor leaves one turf untried,
Till conscious of the recent stains, his heart
Beats quick; his snuffling nose, his active tail,
Attest his joy; then with deep opening mouth,
That makes the welkin tremble, he proclaims
Th'audacious felon; foot by foot he makes
His winding way, while all the listening crowd
Applaud his reasonings: O'er the watery ford,
Dry sandy heaths, and stony barren hills;
O'er beaten paths, by men and beasts disdained,
Unerring he pursues; 'till at the cot
Arrived, and seizing by his guilty throat
The caitif vile, redeems the captive prey.
So exquisitely delicate is his nose.

An early record of the use of what could be loosely termed a Police Dog comes from Luton Bedfordshire. In 1859 Police Officers at Luton had acquired a young bloodhound bitch and were dabbling in the art of 'tracking'.

On Tuesday, 9th August 1859, the body of 21-year old Jane Castle was found on the outskirts of the town, in a chalk pit

THE LIFE, TRIAL, CONFESSION, AND EXECUTION OF
JOSEPH CASTLE,
FOR THE MURDER OF HIS WIFE,
At *LUTON*, on *TUESDAY* the 9th of *AUGUST*, 1859,
Tried and condemned at the BEDFORD ASSIZES, March 14, 1860.

COPY OF VERSES.

Our first blessed parents, blissful placed,
In Eden with all good around,
In perfect innocence they lived,
And peace and happiness they found.
One sole command to them was given,
To taste not that forbidden tree,
Which knowledge give of good and evil,
Or death their certain doom would be.

But Satan, just forced out of heaven,
Sought the new creatures' habitation,
And soon he found Eve's ready ear,
To listen to his smooth oration.
Thus paradise was lost to man,
And misery and death ensued,
By murders foul, disease, and war,
The earth was with dead bodies strew'd.

God a judgments sure will overtake,
All those who break his holy laws,
As Castle's case thus plainly proves,
Then let the wicked timely pause,
A young man here in prime of life,
By evil passions onward led,
To murder her he vowed to love,
And at the sacred altar wed.

Unhappy soon this marriage proved,
No proof that she was false inclin'd,
Unfounded jealousy he felt,
In his excited state of mind.

Fondness and hate alternate found
A place within his boist'rous breast,
The demon Hate the mastery gained,
And suffer'd him to feel no rest.

Now thus to frequent quarrels led,
Which grew to bitterness and strife,
Until from him she fled away,
To 'scape from such unhappy life.
Without or with her ne'er at rest,
He followed to her parents' home,
With promise kind on her prevailed,
That with him back again she'd come.

But when they'd got into a glen,
On the high road, he took her life,
With instrument they used at meals,
Dreadful to think,—a table knife.
A trial fair he surely had,
And all that Counsel could was done,
To Judge and Jury guilt was clear,
Death was his doom—his glass is run.

O awful sight ! a fellow-man,
Hung by the neck to public gaze,
For others to example take,
And check them in their dangerous ways,
And may his fate their warning prove,
'Gainst harbouring malicious thought,
Lead them to pray, for heavenly grace,
That to such end they ne'er be brought.

in Someries Lane. Her throat had been cut and there were other stab wounds to the neck. It also appeared that the murderer had suffered some injury as a trail of blood led away from the scene. Police Superintendent Pope attended the crime and after the body had been taken to a nearby inn (the cellars of such places were often used as mortuaries), summoned the assistance of the Bloodhound. A track was followed for a distance of 2 miles to Welwyn where a man, Joseph Castle, was apprehended. It transpired that this was the husband of the murdered woman. Although there was no evidence of him having been seen with his wife at the time of her murder, the 'track' was accepted as clear proof that he had been at the scene. He also had a cut to the thumb and one finger of his right hand. After an initial denial, Castle broke down and admitted his guilt.

Held in custody for seven months, Joseph Castle eventually stood trial at the Bedford Assizes on March 14 1860 where after a retirement of only 15 minutes the jury returned a verdict of Guilty. A sentence of death by hanging was imposed and at 12 noon Saturday, 31st March 1860 the execution

Broadsheet telling the story of Jane and Joseph Castle.

was carried out on the steps of Bedford Gaol. This spectacle was witnessed by thousands of people who had occupied every conceivable vantage point. (This was the last public execution at Bedford.)

As Police forces came into being, so the use of the dog was eclipsed for some time. However, it had become common practice amongst some officers to take their own dog out with them on night duty. With no formalised training methods, this was quite unofficial, in most cases, and the officer had his dog purely for company and personal protection. For whatever reason, in 1870, Major General G. Allgood CB, Chief Constable of Northumberland instructed his Superintendents to suspend from duty any officer who was found with a dog in his possession, whilst on duty. This restriction was not lifted until 1910.

The author and dog trainer Hugh Dalziel wrote, in 1875:

"I have for many years advocated the training of our bloodhounds as assistants to the police in the detection of crime, and the more I consider the subject by the light of increased experience and knowledge, the more strongly I am convinced that they might be made of the greatest service. Scores of burglaries are committed whilst the family are dining or at church, and discovered very soon; in many cases the thieves are driven hurriedly away, being disturbed before their work is completed, and yet they are rarely caught or afterwards discovered. In country and suburban houses, a bloodhound, or, better, a couple, well trained, would serve at once as deterrents to crime and detectives of the criminals; and such dogs in the hands of the police would be invaluable in putting the latter in the direction the thieves had taken and enable them to trace the miscreants even through crowded streets.

"I have heard no reasons advanced against the use of these dogs, except such as are sentimental and based on misapprehension. People picture to themselves one or more ferocious animals, with glaring bloodshot eyes, running down a criminal and tearing him to pieces, or, to slightly alter a Zulu figure of speech, "washing their tusks", and, it might be, occasionally in the blood of the innocent. Nothing of the kind would or could take place; and even three centuries since, when people were less tender of the sufferings of malefactors, such accidents were rendered impossible by letting the hounds follow the felon, in leash".

Etching from 'Cassell's Illustrated Family Paper', 23 August 1856, showing Petticoat Lane on a Sunday morning. The policeman has his dog for company.

The town of Ghent, in Belgium led the way in the employment of police dogs, as a result of a forward-thinking Police Chief by the name of Van Wesenmael. The following is a letter he wrote to the Mayor of Ghent, in 1890.

Dear Sir – You have permitted me to use all means of experimenting with a night-service of dogs. In presenting you my request for this service, I had in view the number of police doing duty in the outer zone and wood quarters. If we had increased the number of police it would have been a serious expense. Besides, I am not certain that a night policemen, who is acting in the suburbs, far from any help whatever, dare intervene when he sees a crime committed by several criminals. He cannot go as far and as fast as criminals, after being on duty for several hours. The criminal who has been meditating a crime dresses himself in a manner to be working as lightly as possible in case of flight. A dog works a long time on duty cheerfully, and he is able to follow a fugitive much more rapidly than a man. The dog is equipped with qualities of scent and hearing, and can easily get into any place and examine it without his presence being suspected, and thus surprise the ciminal, when the policeman in searching would probably be heard. If the burglar, thanks to his agility, succeeds in jumping over an obstacle or swimming away, a dog can stop him; the policeman would be hampered because of his heavy uniform, and perhaps he could not swim.

What I am anxious to do is to fulfil as completely as possible this want, so as to prevent crimes. Of course, I do not hope to prevent all crimes – that would be an impossibility; we can only unite all our efforts in hindering them. And here one might ask the question as to the night-dog – Is he able to do this? The reports which you find attached answer this question. I am certain that in the future, when the service of night-dogs is organised, it will be still more brilliant. We commenced with three dogs aged one year, then we added two more, and then we increased to ten, and should our ten dogs do good duty, the Municipal Council will soon increase the number of dogs to sixteen; and as I hope this request will be taken up, I propose to assign three dogs to other districts. The future will tell us if we should increase our dogs. If the results continue as satisfactory as they have been up to present, the administration will not have to make any more monetary sacrifices for more policemen for night duty – I remain, yours faithfully,

VAN WESENMAEL

Within a short time, the number of police dogs in Ghent was 69.

Chapter 5

THE FIRST POLICE DOGS
IN ENGLAND

Whilst other continental countries were copying Ghent and, in fact, the use of dogs was spreading worldwide, British police forces shunned the idea. It was not until 1910 that Major Edwin Hautenville Richardson (late 45th Regiment, Sherwood Foresters) wrote to every Chief Constable in the country suggesting the introduction of dogs to assist the 'patrolling constable'.

Major Richardson had a wide knowledge and experience in the training of dogs for the military. He was an acknowledged expert in the use of bloodhounds and had travelled extensively, studying the use of dogs by both army and police. In an interview with the *Liverpool Daily Post* regarding his ideas, he is quoted as saying,

"I think that the Police Authorities may be more inclined to consider the idea when they know that the Admiralty have adopted dogs for watch purposes.

"The dogs I have supplied to the Admiralty are trained to attack a man if necessary. They are being employed on Naval property in England, Ireland and Scotland, and are on duty from ten o'clock at night until six in the morning. During that time they have the free run of the premises. They are chosen from various breeds – cross bred retrievers, Airedales and sheepdogs, and crosses between sheepdogs and retrievers. They have special qualities fitting them for their work.

"What I want to do now is to convince the Police that the system of employing dogs, which is followed in France and Germany, is not silly, but really useful. The Berlin authorities have just voted £1,350 for the extension of the system. M. Lepine, the French Minister of Police, is very keen on the use of dogs for

police purposes at night. It is recognised abroad that
such dogs are a powerful deterrent to burglars, as well as
extremely useful in capturing them. The practice is
to keep them muzzled until occasion arises for
unmuzzling them.

"In the suburbs of London, where burglaries are
always being committed, I believe that if the night
policemen had dogs with them the number of
burglaries would rapidly diminish. In Berlin there has
been a drop of 35% in crimes since dogs were
introduced.

"It is hard to convince Scotland Yard but with the
Admiralty as witness I think it is a much more hopeful
outlook. The Admiralty are so satisfied that they have
given me orders for some more dogs".

As a direct result of this letter some Chief Constables, including the Chief Constable of Nottingham City Police took
the advice given. Extracts taken from reports of various Nottingham City Watch Committee meetings at the Guildhall
give the following summary:

23 March 1910
The Chief Constable reported a letter from Major
Richardson, as to the use of Police Dogs and
recommended that the committee should have a dog
trained as an experiment at a cost of £5.0.0d. It was
agreed.

26 October 1910
The Chief Constable reported that the trained Police
Dog obtained from Major Richardson, in accordance
with the order of the committee, has arrived.

8 February 1911
The Chief Constable reported that the Police Dog still
continued to improve in his work, was in good health
and found to be exceedingly useful to the Police.

Chief Constable's Annual Report 1910
The Police Dog is a distinct acquisition to the Force,
particularly in connection with the night patrolling of
outside districts. He is a powerful and sensible animal,
and is being regularly exercised and trained in his
work. He has proved himself most useful in finding
persons secreted in out of the way places, and he has
followed and stopped others at some distance away

By kind permission of the London News Agency.

First English Official Police Dog, supplied to the Berkshire Police by Major Richardson.

whom the police were desirous of overhauling, but would have failed to get into touch with without the dogs' assistance.

Although the photograph above is captioned 'First English Official Police Dog', this dog had not been purchased until 1911, some time after Nottingham City's first experimental dog. Berkshire Constabulary's own records state:

In 1911 Sir Theodore Brinckman, a large landowner, purchased one of Major Richardsons' police dogs and presented it to Clewer Police Station; we were

therefore one of the first police forces in the country to
secure an executive dog for night duty with a policeman.
The dog was a cross between a Labrador and a Retriever
and was called "Nigger". He served the Force for a number
of years and although no conspicuous "arrests" came his
way, he was soon found to be a deterring factor to any
would-be law breaker.

From that time onwards this Force made little use of dogs but,
on the few occasions the need did arise, they were borrowed
either from neighbouring forces or suitable private breeders.

The extracts that follow are from Nottingham City Watch
Committee reports:

12 April 1911

The Chief Constable reported that the Police Dog had
proved very satisfactory and useful, and that Major
Richardson had informed him that he would be able
to supply other suitable dogs if required. It was
resolved that 2 more dogs would be purchased.

13 September 1911

The Chief Constable reported that one of the Police
Dogs had been poisoned as a result of a resident in
The Park, Nottingham, throwing poisoned meat into
the garden of an empty house, which was patrolled by
the Police. The dog had died and the man, Mr.
Charles Gregory of The Park, had paid the Police the
value of the dog. It was resolved that another dog be
obtained.

8 November 1911

Mr Charles Gregory was requested to pay Dr.
Trotmans' account for the analysis, with reference to
the poisoning of the Police Dog.

26 June 1912

Another dog has been obtained from Major
Richardson with an account for £5.12s.6d.

25 June 1913

Police Dog Duke had arrived and the price of
£1.0s.0d. had been paid. [Details of breed and
supplier not known.]

The combined hindrance of sceptics and the little use of
police dogs already in service, prompted Sir Leonard

A family album photograph showing PC Robinson with Police Dog Duke.

Dunning, HM Inspector of Constabulary, in 1913, to report to the Secretary of State:

> On the continent of Europe where dogs are largely used by the police, their physical aid in overtaking and securing offenders is regarded in a somewhat different light to what it would be in this country, with the result that the dogs are much larger than those used here, and that they are kept muzzled until the moment for action.

Also in that year Lieutenant-Colonel John Eden, Inspector of Constabulary reported:

> An interesting experiment is being made by Major

Bower, the Chief Constable of the Northern Riding of Yorkshire in utilising dogs for police work. At the present time about 20% of the force are permitted to keep and use their own dogs. These animals are chiefly Airedale Terriers and are carefully trained for the work. They are useful in accompanying the individual constable when on night patrol both for protection and companionship, and a help to him especially on dark nights in bringing to notice things that might otherwise escape his attention. Airedale Terriers have also for some time now been used by the police in the outlying parts of the City of Liverpool, and have proved to be a success.

It was also noted at this time Major Llewellyn Atcherley, the Chief Constable of the West Riding of Yorkshire, likewise gave active support to any of his officers wishing to train and use a dog to assist them.

The following is a North Riding of Yorkshire Police Order dated March 20th, 1914.

NORTH RIDING POLICE BLOODHOUNDS

Telegrams – Fox, Police, Thirsk
Telephone – No P.O.12, Thirsk

Address of Officer in charge
Detective Sergeant Fox
Police Station
Thirsk

RULES TO BE OBSERVED

(1) Wire or telephone for bloodhounds immediately the crime is discovered. The more delay, the less scent.

(2) Do not let it be known that bloodhounds are coming.

(3) Keep the scene of the crime clear of people for as great a distance around as possible. If in a field, park, or wood, keep all ingresses closed. If in a house keep everyone from door or window by which criminal has left.

(4) Criminals rarely leave anything behind; therefore keep a careful watch for footprints and cover the same with boards, box or boxes. This will keep in the scent.

(5) Make a careful note of the trail of (1st) the discoverer of the crime (2nd) of that of the first policeman on the spot (3rd) of any other persons that of necessity must visit the scene, until the hounds arrive. It must be clearly understood that the fewer persons inspecting the spot the better until Hounds arrive.

Bloodhounds being given a scent.

(6) The Hounds will arrive by motor car.

R.L. BOWER, MAJOR
Chief Constable,
North Riding of Yorkshire

In May 1914 Major Richardson addressed members of the Chief Constables (Cities and Boroughs) Association at Grimsby, on the use of dogs as aids to the Police Service. Explaining all the attributes of the dog, he also defined two types of Police Dog:

The Night Patrol Dog — with duties:
1. To go out ahead of the Policemen, as a scout.

2. To scent out and give warning of any suspicious person who may be lying hidden in gardens, lanes, parks, etc.
3. To protect the Policemen from attack.
The Criminal Tracking Dog – with the sole duty of 'tracking' an offender.

Although Bloodhounds were owned by one or two Chief Constables, Major Richardson advocated the use of Airedales in both situations.

A further extract from the Nottingham City Watch Committee:

22 July 1914
 Police Dog Ben has been retired through lameness and
 an Airedale Terrier is to be purchased from Mr Wing
 of North Road, Maltby, Yorkshire for the sum of
 £3.3s.0d.

Also in the year of 1914, 172 Constables in the Metropolitan Police were given authority to take their own dogs on duty with them. The licences were paid from official funds, but there was still no real training programme. This system continued through the First World War until 1931 when it was decided that, for economy's sake, the Constables' dog licences would no longer be paid from official funds. The number of dogs had dropped to 37 by that year and dropped to 12 by 1937.

Nottingham City Watch Committee:

23 December 1914
 An Airedale Terrier dog has been presented for Police
 Purposes by Mr. James Hickinbottom of Fern Dale,
 West Bridgford, Nottingham, as a 'gift'

On a lighter note, the following entry appeared in the Police Diary, at Canal Street Police Station, in Nottingham, on 25th June, 1916:

 PC 308 Tuckwood reports that at 1.30am on the 22nd
 instant, when in Sneinton Dale, he lost Police Dog
 Prince from the Hermitage Beat. It was later found by
 Inspector Bingham at Fisher Gate. This is not the first
 time this has occurred, and considerable time is wasted
 in waiting for this dog. The dog appears to have bad
 feet, taking every facility for sitting down during the
 night.

The only recorded incident, during the War years, when dogs were used by the police comes by way of the *Camberley News*, dated 30th September 1916, which reported that five Prisoners of War, four sailors and an aircraftsman had escaped from a working party whilst returning to Frith Hill Camp, Surrey. A hue and cry was immediately raised and Sergeant Kenward from Camberley attended with three Bloodhounds. The hounds tracked the men as far as Brookwood where all trace was lost. Three prisoners were subsequently caught, the following day, but there was no further mention of the dogs.

Nottingham City Watch Committee:

12 December 1917
    The Chief Constable has reported that a new Police Dog has been received at the cost of £2.7s.2d. from Sgt Arundel of Settle which included its training, upkeep and rail fare.

27 March 1918
    Ilkeston Road Police Dog has been diagnosed as unfit for further work by a Vet and has been destroyed.

10 April 1918
    Police Dog Prince had become unfit and unwell and had been destroyed. It was resolved that a new type of dog, 'the Dog-Wolf' be obtained and trained.

The latter description of the German Shepherd no doubt should have read the 'wolf-dog'.

8 May 1918
    A letter was read from Lady Helen Conyhgham offering, at the price of 12 guineas, two more of the same dogs as the one recently purchased from her [wolf-dog/Alsatian/German Shepherd]. It was resolved that the two dogs be purchased.

22 May 1918
    Police Dog Don had defective eyesight and become too old for work and had been destroyed.

12 June 1918
    A report was read by the Veterinary Surgeon as to the filthy condition in which the pups, recently purchased, were found to be in when received, and also a letter

48

from Lady McCalmont expressing regret that the pups
had arrived in this condition which she stated was due
to her inability to give them her personal attention.
The pups were now being attended to.

9 October 1918

Report from the Vet that one of the two wolf-hound
pups, recently purchased for Police work, had died
from distemper. The other pup was in good health.

No further mention of Police Dogs is found at these meetings
until the mid-1950s, when Police Dog Sections were being
formed nationwide. It would appear that many Police
Authorities showed little interest in the use of dogs following
the end of the war in 1918. However, there would still
appear to be one or two remaining active, by virtue of the
following extracts from Nottingham City Police records: –

Canal Street Police Station

From Insp. Bingham
re: Police dog 'JACK'

June 1920
To: Patrol P.c.

A dog is now kept at this station for Police Patrol.
Men on 14 beat Night Duty will take him out for
about 2 or 3 hours between 1.30pm and 4am, if fine.
  1st relief P.c. take him out.
  3rd relief P.c. also take him out about 2 hrs.
  Should he get wet an old towel hangs on the coal
place door and he must be rubbed dry. P.c's will be
held responsible that he is not played with or
encouraged to chase cats etc.

Police Dog Jack gained some notoriety in that on 9th May
1923 the Chief Constable reported that this dog had bitten
Cyril Attenborough of 9, Dale Street, Nottingham and that
the boy had been off work for a short time. The matter had
been resolved, without admitting liability, in that
Attenborough was granted a gratuity of £4.4s.0d.
  The Nottingham City Chief Constable Annual General
Reports for 1910/14/18 indicate the strength of Police Dogs
to have been 1, 6 and 4 respectively. Details of Police Dogs
were then, for reasons unknown, omitted from subsequent
reports until 1954.

In 1919 Superintendent Reginal Arundel, West Riding Constabulary began writing articles on the training of police dogs in an effort to stimulate further interest, culminating in a book titled *Police Dogs and their Training,* (mainly adpted from a German book, by Gerbach, the translation rights of which he had purchased before the war).

It is interesting to note the desirable qualities, as outlined in the book, when assessing a puppy:

He is seen to be sharp and courageous if he
1. Attacks cats
2. Barks madly at them
3. Attacks other dogs
4. Barks at strangers
5. Goes for the legs of tramps
6. Wags his tail when feeding and will not allow other dogs or animals to approach; raises his hair and growls when disturbed.

Prior to being allowed to attempt any criminal work (namely biting, under control) the dog had to show the following qualities and accomplishments: –

1. Implicit obedience to the handler
2. Undoubted courage
3. To follow at heel and to act as leader when unleashed
4. To bark at command
5. To refuse food from a strangers' hand
6. To fetch and carry, both in and out of the water and over obstacles
7. To jump at least 5 feet high
8. Perfect steadiness under gunfire
9. To search premises and give tongue on finding person concealed
10. To defend his master
11. To follow up, throw down, hold fast and give tongue
12. To carry reports to the Police Station, or to an officer in charge
13. By means of the scent, to discover and follow up a mans' track, and search for stolen property.

To acquire the title of 'Police Dog', the dog was trained through a total of 83 separate exercises and expected to be proficient in each.

During this and the following years numerous breeds of

dogs were tried and tested including the Great Dane, Airedale Terrier, Mastiff, Bull-Mastiff, Retriever, Kerry Blue Terrier and the Dobermann Pinscher. The Alsatian Wolf Dog (German Shepherd) was somewhat new to Britain and being treated with some suspicion and disdain, although by the mid-1920s it topped the polls as the most popular breed.

In an effort to promote the 'gamekeepers favourite', the Bull-Mastiff, as a breed specific for the purpose, in 1925 the National Bull-Mastiff Police Dog Club was founded. Described as faithful, fearless but not ferocious, with a good nose for tracking, it was thought the breed would be a success.

Detective Chief Superintendent Tom Roberts of the Surrey Constabulary recognised the potential of using bloodhounds for police work in 1933. After convincing his Chief Constable of their value, a PC Potter who was stationed at Ash and the owner of two such dogs was approached and given the opportunity to train and use them for police duties. PC Potter gave valued service until 1938 and, although not credited with any arrests, the team were responsible for finding clues at the scenes of crime, finding missing persons and retrieving discarded stolen property.

Tom Roberts continued his interest in the use of police dogs after the war and was instrumental in the formation of the Surrey Police Dog Training School.

In 1934 a Home Office Committee (examing Detective Work and Procedure) examined the value of dogs to the police service, together with facilities and training requirements. Extreme prejudice was rife against the use of dogs, and the members met with some hostility. However after considering a report by a Metropolitan officer, on the use of police dogs by some continental forces he had visited, the decision was taken to carry out experiments in breeding and training dogs, with the aim of developing a suitable breed for tracking and general protective purposes.

Mr. H.S. Lloyd of Swakeleys Farm, Ickenham, Middlesex, a renowned gun dog breeder and trainer, was called in and began experiments, with a paid annual subsidy of £500 to conduct them. These experiments ended on the outbreak of the Second World War in 1939 but not before Mr. Lloyd had given the result of his findings in an address *The Value of Dogs to the Police,* at the Chief Constables' Association Conference at Cambridge. He described, in detail, his experiments with various breeds but added a rider about the Alsatian: "Public opinion was rather aginst the use of these and the Committee dealing with this matter wisely refrained from making use of them."

During this experimental period and following an interim report, in 1935, from the Committee, by 1938 the Metropolitan Police had trained two Labradors which, together with their handlers were posted to the Crime Squad in South London. However, this came to a dramatic halt with the onset of the War and the dogs were handed over to the Cheshire Constabulary.

Tom Scott, the author of *Obedience and Security Training for Dogs,* joined the Metropolitan Police in 1929 and quickly became one of the many officers who took a dog out with them on night duty, mainly for company. He relates that during those years before the Second World War, policing was quite informal, as long as the officer was 'working his beat' he could use anything that would be of assistance, even a horse and cart. Posted to Staines, Middlesex, in 1934, Tom acquired Ruby, an Alsatian bitch pup that was later to prove a real pal by accompanying him on patrol either on foot or running beside his pedal cycle. Sadly this companionship only lasted until she was 18 months old when she was put to sleep due to the disease distemper.

A short time afterwards Tom replaced Ruby with Juno a 12-month old Alsatian dog who, by all accounts, rarely let Tom out of his sight. One one occasion, after only being with the family three days, Juno broke free from being exercised to travel some distance away to join Tom who was regulating traffic in the middle of the High Street. Juno was to remain in the down position in a shop doorway until the arrival of a police wireless car which took the dog home. Although not credited with any actual arrests Juno was a great deterrent and saved Toms' neck in many an encounter with gypsies.

Tom continued through the war years without a dog because, in his own words "There was no meat to feed them with". He subsequently joined the newly emerging Metropolitan Police Dog Section in 1947 to continue working and training dogs.

Samuel Robinson joined the Nottinghamshire Constabulary on 10th March 1919, at the age of 24. He was later to be stationed at Welbeck, a village on the estate of the Duke of Portland. The area suffers from poachers to this day, but was notorious at that time. PC Robinson was supplied, by the Duke, with three Bull Mastiffs to assist him in the apprehension of poachers. Their upkeep was also paid for by the

Duke. These dogs not only assisted the officer and gamekeepers on the land but were also known to keep the peace at the local hostelries.

Knowledge of PC Robinson's dog handling abilities reached the ears of the Chief Constable Colonel F.J. Lemon, who, reacting to an epidemic of burglaries at Arnold, Nottingham, transferred PC Robinson to that station, requesting him to handle an official Police Dog.

Colonel Lemon had previously addressed the Nottinghamshire Standing Joint Committee at a meeting on 22nd April 1938 with the following; "The Home Office have for some time past been experimenting with dogs suitable for Police Work. As a result they now report that the most suitable dog for such work is the Labrador and they have a certain number of these trained and ready for disposal to Police Forces at a cost of £12.0.0d. I beg to ask the sanction of the Committee to purchase one of these dogs and to make an allowance of 3/6d per week for its upkeep." The matter was resolved and agreed.

After attending a three week training course with Mr. Lloyd, PC Robinson returned home in June 1938 with a 4-year old black Labrador dog, Duke. Although the property of the Chief Constable, the dog was kept at the officer's home and the agreed allowance of 3/6d (17½p) paid weekly for food. Colonel Lemon attended a demonstration of the dogs' ability and upon hearing that the dog was to be used for night duty insisted that a coat be tailor-made and a commitment given that it be used to keep the dog warm and dry. The crime wave abated and the team were later transferred to West Bridgford, in 1939, to combat further burglaries. After service throughout the war Duke died in 1946, not to be replaced. Old habits die hard and it was well known that Duke was as well trained to 'the gun' as he was to detecting criminals.

One of the main reasons why no dogs were used by the police in the war years was that in 1940 all dogs within the British Isles were invited to register for national service. Only those of certain breeds and with natural qualifications of a high order would be recruited. Their duties included guarding installations and mine detection. Airedales, Collies (both rough and smooth), Hill Collies, Crossbreds, Lurchers and Retrievers (Labrador and Golden) were the most suitable kinds, but members of other breeds would be considered provided that their intelligence and natural ability were of a superior standard. It was presumed that friendly aliens, such as the Alsatian, would not be turned down through prejudice. Accepted candidates were given an intensive course of training at Willems Barracks, Aldershot. Dogs which failed to pass the tests were immediately returned home. Successful dogs were to serve in the army for the duration of the war, receiving skilled care and attention.

These dogs were classed as only being 'on loan' from their patriotic owners, to be returned upon cessation of hostilities. Thus, this official request plus the scarcity of dog food effectively kept suitable dogs out of civilian police hands. The 'everyday' dog population, however, did not alter that much, in 1939 there were 2,800,000 dogs and in February 1944 an estimated 2,400,000.

Through the war years nothing more was heard, until 1946 when with a rising crime rate in the capital, generally attributed to the returning armies, interest was renewed in the use of dogs to assist the Metropolitan Police. As a result, under the direction of Assistant Commissioner Captain Rhymer Jones, PC Charles Stephenson travelled to York and collected four Labrador puppies for future training. These dogs were teamed:

Sergeant Boath with Jim
PC Laidlaw with Prince
PC James with Garry
PC Shelton with Jess.

While these pups were growing PC Stephenson, together with his family, was sent to live in Essex with Captain J. Kent, late of the Army War Dog School, at his dog training establishment at Audely End.

With a Labrador dog, Squire, purchased by the police from Captain Kent, PC Stephenson spent the next nine months under training and was, in his own words, "considered to be the Dog Trainer", when he returned to police duties.

It was decided, from the beginning, if the scheme was to succeed, each dog was to work with the same handler and live with him at his home and also, to prevent claims about the wrong person being bitten, the dogs would not be trained to bite the fleeing criminal but to get in front of him and to turn and bark to prevent further escape.

With all the dogs trained to this standard it quickly became apparent that changes had to be made after the following incident:

At 1.30am PC Stephenson was patrolling Hyde Park, in plain clothes, when his dog Squire was sent in pursuit of a suspect. The dog quickly caught up with him but undeterred the villain kept on running, out onto Park Lane. The pursuit continued with the dog jumping up but failing to have any effect. PC Stephenson managed to flag down a passing taxi cab and with the aid of the driver managed to catch the man and make an arrest. The suspect subsequently admitted numerous handbag thefts that night.

A concession was made and from that point the dogs, although still in theory not allowed to bite, were allowed to take hold of the right coat sleeve.

By August 1947, although little impact had been made, the establishment was increased by one Sergeant and two Constables. The Sergeant handling a Labrador, Sam, with PC Scott handling cross-bred Collie, Pluto and PC Albert Blake handling Labrador, Ping. In general the Dog Section were regarded with amused intolerance or hostility and unless better results were obtained by these new additions, the 'dog experiment' would be abandoned. Within weeks of their completed training, whilst stationed at Surbiton, Surrey, PC Blake and Ping were to effect the arrest of two men which gained commendations from both the Court and the Commissioner, the first awarded for work involving a Police Dog. The result was that instructions were given that police dog teams were to be called to any incident where they might prove useful.

To quote PC Blakes' own recollections of the arrest in December 1947:

"Some time after midnight we kept under observation two men whose apearance did not fit in with the wealthy neighbourhood they were in. Losing sight of the men − there was no street lighting − at the junction of five roads, I took Ping down the nearest road ordering him to 'Seek' with a negative result, as was the case in a search for the next road. Returning to the crossroads I placed the dog on a long tracking lead and with a further command to 'Seek' left it to him. Without hesitation he raced across the junction and through the broken fence of a large garden surrounding a house called Croylands. His eagerness left no doubt we were close to our quarry − dodging trees in the dark at the end of a tracking lead following a dog with breast high scent has its problems. Passing close to us in the dark the men returned to the road where I stopped them. A brief search of one of them yielded a screwdriver and file. With some reluctance which was overcome by Ping's

PC Albert Blake with Ping.

obvious interest in them, they came with us to
Surbiton Police Station where a more thorough search
found a toy pistol and they were charged with being
on enclosed premises and possessing housebreaking
implements. The sequel came later in the morning

when a servant in a house, opposite to where I had
stopped the men, reported it had been broken into and
a valuable Persian carpet stolen. Footprints in the
garden of the house matched those made by one of the
men. The carpet was found in the garden of Croylands
and the men were then further charged with burglary
and sentenced to two years at the Surrey Quarter
Sessions."

The importance of the contribution made by a Police Dog,
a major factor in the case, lay in the fact that they were then
very much on trial and under adverse scrutiny. It is extremely
sad to note that by 1950, and again in his own words
"disillusioned with the prevailing policy towards Police
Dogs" PC Blake resigned from the Dog Section and his dog
Ping was disposed of by the police to a building firm at Mit-
cham, as a guard dog. Anxious as to his dog's welfare PC
Blake endeavoured, after seeing the dog and being affec-
tionately greeted by it, to gain ownership but this was only
rewarded with the dog being put down. Certainly not a
fitting end to one of the founders of the Dog Section!

Albert Blake recalls an amusing incident where he and Ping
were asked to perform a display at Imber Court (Headquarters of the Metropolian Police Athletic Association) in
front of dignitaries, including the Commissioner and the
Prefect of the Paris Police and their ladies. The team were to
demonstrate the dog's ability in apprehending a handbag
thief. The scene was set, other dog handlers dressed as the
thief and a lady, and the 'snatch' took place. Albert emerged
from nearby bushes, challenged the thief who refused to
stop, and Ping was released in pursuit. As the dog took hold
of the thief's right arm, to make it look better, our villain
swung Ping off his feet and then made to kick him. Unfor-
tunately the pretend kick connected with Ping's underside
whereupon he promptly let go of the arm and reattached
himself to the mans' chest, knocking him to the ground. With
screams of pain and cries for help our villain was applauded
by the ladies with shouts of "Bravo, well done"; the display
was completed and our man quickly taken away. The ladies
before leaving, expressed the desire to see the wonderful
actor and congratulate him on his performance. Excuses
were made to the effect that he had been called away on
police business, rather than say he was detained at the local
hospital.

During 1947 Chief Superintendent H.S. Kemble of

Southampton Borough Police, together with other officers, visited Denmark to assess the use of police dogs in that country. As a result he was converted and the following is from a report he submitted upon his return:

> If police dogs are ever extensively used in England the experiment will fail from the beginning unless proper attention is given first of all to the importation of the most useful breed from reputed stock. Then training, training and more training, and practical work and use. At present in this country we appear to impose too much responsibility on the CID to detect all offences, but 50 per cent of crime is undetectable and should, by preventive measures, be put beyond the reach of the wrongdoer in the beginning. Countless business houses are shamelessly insecure, but until building regulations require a degree of security for valuable goods, dogs are the answer to the problem. The most sceptical of us agreed that it would be difficult to imagine an area where police work could not be carried out better by the employment of dogs, if only from the preventive aspects".

Also in 1947 Mr Joseph Simpson, Chief Constable of Surrey and member of the Kennel Club, having already shown great interest in 'working dogs' now focused his attention on training dogs for police work. Mr Simpson knew of a PC Darbyshire who was working in the Criminal Records Office at Scotland Yard. This officer had considerable knowledge of continental police dog training and breeding methods but showed little interest in the Metropolitan Police dog section owing to the fact that they used Labradors, not Alsatians and they were not susceptible to his ideas.

With the agreement of the Commissioner of the Metropolitan Police and the Home Office, PC Darbyshire was offered a transfer with the rank of Sergeant, which he accepted. He took with him his fully trained Alsatian bitch, Anne of Avondale (ex German war dog no 1758X1 – captured by a Corporal Ken Bailey, Parachute Regiment near Ashwerin, Germany, in 1945). Sergeant Darbyshire's brief was to formulate a police dog section using the continental system of training, employing only the Alsatian and Dobermann breeds.

Police forces nationally were now taking note and carrying out their own experiments. In 1949 the Metropolitan Police opened the first dog training school at Imber Court. This was a sports ground at Thames Ditton which was also used as the headquarters of the Metropolitan Police Athletic Association. The area allocated to the dogs was too small and

Facing page: 'Tailwagger' was a popular magazine in the 1940s and 50s, filled with doggy stories and advice on pet care. In 1956 Police Dog Hagen was enrolled in the Tail-Waggers' Club as a "true friend", Tail-Wagger number 998942.

"SAFE RETURN, DAD !" The P.C. leaves home for duty, accompanied by his Police Dog (*See story on page* 111)

Training course at Keston, 1955.

because of daily games meetings there was no special area the dog handlers could call their own. The kennels were badly constructed and inadequate and the only breed of dog authorised was the Labrador. The Alsatian was unacceptable to the general public of the London area due to its supposedly unpredictable temperament.

On the 27th September 1950 Surrey opened its own Police Dog training school and kennels at Headquarters, Mountbrowne, Guildford.

In the initial stages the two schools were seen to be going their own different ways: Surrey, a County Constabulary, giving more attention to nose-work and tracking and the metropolis concentrating more on the criminal man-work (the old concept of tracker dog and patrol dog). These principles were to be quickly discarded and the all-encompassing general purpose dog evolved.

By 1952 Imber Court had opened its kennel doors to all breeds, including the Alsatian, but by virtue of the increase in numbers and noise these premises were now becoming unacceptable. Disease was also prevalent as, by June 1951, 19 dogs had died of distemper.

On 16th June 1954 the present Metropolitan Police Dog

Training Centre at Keston, Kent was officially opened by Sir
John Nott-Bower, the dogs numbered:

Alsatians	128
Labradors	9
Dobermanns	2
German Pointer	1

Exactly one week later the kennels were closed and all training suspended due to an outbreak of distemper. Many
trainee and working dogs had to be destroyed as the disease
spread. This was almost certainly due to the practice of not
innoculating police dogs on the grounds of expense and bad
veterinary advice. Fortunately Mr A.B. McIntyre, MRCVS,
of the Burroughs and Wellcome Research Laboratory,
Beckenham, Kent came to the rescue. The disease was
eradicated and as a result of his advice, by 1956 hygienic
methods and an innoculation programme were established
and necessary building alterations were completed.

By 1954 most of the larger police forces had set up Dog
Sections and an enormous number of dogs were being used.
However, their progress depended on the suitability of
trainers and the enthusiasm of Chief Constables. Owing to
the wide variation of standards there was a distinct need for
some kind of common policy and, therefore, the Association
of Chief Police Officers appointed a working party to study
the whole problem. A total of 28 of the 126 British Police
Forces, were using, between them, 266 dogs.

In 1955 it was agreed amongst the training schools then in
operation that training programmes would be prepared to
bring out the full qualities of the dog in searching, tracking
and man-work, whilst still keeping the dog under the
complete control of the handler.

Locally, Nottingham City officers were sent to Keston for
their training, whereas Nottinghamshire officers were sent to
Surrey. One such Nottinghamshire officer was PC 182
Sydenham who had always seen the potential of dogs being
used by the police. In 1955, whilst walking his beat at
Hucknall, he saw two Dobermann pups being walked along
the High Street. The following day, after a lot of bartering,
with a £1.00 deposit and 17 further £1.00 weekly payments
(money, I am assured, was short in those days) he became the
proud owner of Starke, one of the Dobermann dog pups.

When the dog was 6 months old PC Sydenham tried, in
vain on two occasions, to be allowed to take the dog out with
him on night duty. However, when the dog was about 11
months of age an instruction came from the Chief Constable

PC Sydenham with Wotan, the First Police Dog I saw in action as a young Constable, although he was then handled by PC John Rebaudi (see page 10).

J.E.S. Browne for PC Sydenham and Starke to attend a dog training course at Guildford, Surrey. Sergeant Harry Darbyshire had, by this time, built up a formidable breeding programme centred at Mountbrowne with dogs being supplied nationwide on condition that they be returned, at any time, for breeding purposes under his watchful eye and only he had access to records kept. (When Sergeant Darbyshire retired in November 1959 he, for whatever reason, destroyed all of his breeding records).

PC Sydenham completed what was then a two-stage course with Starke, although the dog had not been favoured because it was not of Mountbrowne stock. PC Sydenham well remembers the fact that Harry Darbyshire maintained that a time restricted training course was stupid, with the quote "You can pour a half pint of ale into a pint glass, Taff, but you can't pour a pint of ale into a half pint glass, it will overflow". He believed the length of the training course should be flexible to accommodate the varying abilities of each dog.

As an operational handler, PC Sydenham returned to Nottinghamshire where the kennels were situated in the old stables at Headquarters, Epperstone Manor. The section steadily increased in number, their main call out was to search for abscondees from nearby Lowdham Borstal. The means of transport was the groundsman's 15cwt ex-army truck which was commandeered, grass clippings and all, with dogs tied to the tarpaulin support bars. Those early days were described as crude – but happy.

Around this time, there was an amusing incident after the Chief Constable had ordered the section to be issued with distinctive clothing to assist them in their duties. This consisted of knee breeches, believed to date back to the motorcycling era of the 1930s, which had been gathering dust in the stores and were well-described as of the bulbous type worn by the Gestapo, tied just below the knee with laces. There was no mention of, or supply of, gaiters or high boots. On the day of issue the officers were told the Chief was going to inspect the kennels and they were to wear the new breeches.

Training course in Surrey, 1956.

The officers stood, in a line, with breeches on, bare legs

from the knee down, one had red socks, another blue, others were black, white etc, some wore shoes, others boots. When the Chief came, all stood to attention trying to look as serious as possible. The Chief just looked, shook his head and without saying a word turned and walked away, trying not to laugh. Exit the breeches.

Until 1958 each force had continued to do its own thing but from then on all knowledge, experience and problems were to be tackled on a national basis, with three major issues to be considered, the type of dog required, the selection of handler, and the training of both. As a result of the Working Party of 1954, in March 1958 the Home Office Standing Advisory Committee on Police Dogs was established, to guide and advise throughout the country. Following this, National Police Dog Trials were initiated with the purpose of encouraging the maintenance and improvement of standards. A comprehensive training manual titled *Police Dogs – Training and Care* was published in 1963.

In 1964 a National Course for Instructors was set up, piloted by an experienced police dog trainer from Germany.

In 1965 Sir Edward Dodds, CBE, QPM, HM Chief Inspector of Constabulary said: "Reports from Chief Constables, prove beyond doubt the efficiency of the trained dog and its importance to the Police Service . . . it is as a deterrent that the Police Dog is most useful, and its value in preventing crime can never be assessed . . . mans' oldest friend, the dog, is still proving he is worth his weight in gold in many situations".

Chapter 6

SPECIALIST SEARCH DOGS

Until recently Specialist Search Dogs were picked from the ranks of the normal working police dog, having already shown an above average ability in the art of 'nosework'. However, problems were found in the ability of the dog to be able to switch roles.

At the time of these 'dual-role' police dogs, nearly all were of the German Shepherd breed. Having learned 'criminal work' in its early training and still working the streets as an operational dog, it was extremely hard for the dog to change into a placid searcher, ignoring what he would normally be expected to take note of i.e., one moment being expected to search for any article bearing human scent, the next ignoring that and only searching for the special scent. The dog was also expected to continue searching through the hysteria that sometimes accompanied the forceful entry of premises and the distracting conduct of people inside. Therefore breeds of dog of hardworking and placid type were introduced and trained for one specific role.

Drug Detection

The first police dog to be trained in drug detection is credited to the Israeli Police who trained their dog called Lassie to seek out cannabis in 1950.

The first dog in Great Britain was a Metropolitan Police Dog, Rex 111, handled by PC Arthur Holman who demonstrated his skills on the 17th November 1953 to the satisfaction of, what was then, the Narcotics Branch of the Home Office. From early beginnings in the detection solely of cannabis, specialist dogs now being trained are capable of detecting all the common drugs.

Explosive Detection

In 1968 Mr Melbourne Thomas, Chief Constable of Glamorgan, South Wales, fearing the work of political extremists at the forthcoming investiture of HRH Prince

Charles as the Prince of Wales, assumed that if dogs could detect drugs then they could equally be employed in the detection of explosives. Implementing a training programme, with the assistance of the Bomb Disposal Unit at Chester, PC 309 Sydenham with his yellow Labrador Sandy became operational and were declared a success. It is interesting to note that PC Sydenham was the same officer who was the first 'operational handler' of the Nottinghamshire Constabulary, in 1956 with his Dobermann dog Starke, having resigned from that Force and joined the Welsh Constabulary in 1963.

Buried Body Detection

In 1969 the Lancashire Constabulary Dog Training School began an 18-month training programme in the detection of buried bodies using Tess, a Border Collie and Carl, a German Shepherd dog. The primary use of these dogs was for the detection of human bodies, but it must be understood that the training only used the carcasses of pigs. The true success of this macabre training was later to be revealed at the end of the 1973 Arab Israeli War when five of these dogs, together with their handlers, went to the Sinai Desert and were responsible for locating 147 human remains.

PC Sydenham with Explosive Search Dog Bonnie.

Chapter 7

SCENT AND TRACKING

The study of scent, and the art of tracking, is nothing new. Man and dog have worked together since man made his first kill. As early as AD200 an early Christian zoologist, Oppian, wrote:

> When some hunter wishes to make trials of his dogs, he carries in his hands a hare, dead or alive, and walks forward in a devious path, now pursung a straight course, now aslant, left or right twining his crooked way, but when he has come far from the gates of the city, he digs a trench and buries the hare. Returning to the city, he straightway brings near the path the cunning dog and immediately it is excited at the scent of the hare and seeks the track upon the ground. When at least he hits the airy trail, he gives tongue and whines with joy.

What, I ask, was the dog 'tracking' the scent of the hare or of his owner? William Somerville, the first writer to throw any real light on the subject of scent, wrote in 1742:

> Should some more curious sportsmen here inquire
> Whence this sagacity, this wondrous power
> of tracing step by step of man or brute?
> What guide invisible points out their way
> O'er the dank marsh, bleak hill, and sandy plain?
> The courteous muse shall the dark cause reveal
> The blood that from the heart incessant rolls
> In many a crimson tide, then here and there
> In smaller rills disparted, as it flows
> Propell'd, the serous particles evade
> Thro' the open'd pores, and with the ambient air
> Entangling mix. As fuming vapours rise
> and hang upon the gently purling brook,

67

there by the incumbent atmosphere compress'd,
The panting chase grows warmer as he flies,
And through the network of the skin perspires,
Leaves a long, steaming trail behind; which by
The cooler air condensed, remains unless
By some rude storm dispersed, or rarefied
By the meridian sun's intense heat.
To every shrub the warm effluvia cling,
Hang on the grass, impregnate earth and skies
With nostrils opening wide, o'er hill, o'er dale
The vig'rous hounds pursue, with every breath
Inhale the grateful steam, quick pleasures sting
Their tingling nerves, while they their thanks repay
And in triumphant melody confess
The titillating joy. Thus on the air
Depend the hunters' hopes.

The sense of smell is governed, in animals, by the olfactory gland – the nose. The scent-detecting part is the olfactory mucous membrane and it is the size of this membrane which denotes how great has been the need for this sense during its own evolutionary process. As can be seen from the skull of the dog, and others of the canine family, fullest use of this sense has developed, given the relative size of the nose, compared with our own. For a dog to detect and follow a line of scent is as natural to him as eating and needs no teaching. What we do in training is to give the dog the incentive to follow a particular scent to its origin.

Scent is a fascinating subject and a multi-million pound industry for those who create it for fashion. Scientists are able to re-create any type of smell from chemical compounds and I have experienced a book of smells, developed for blind people, which can give up the smell of new mown grass, farmyard manure, a bonfire or spring meadow etc. simply by sniffing a page, or bottle.

What is scent? It is an odour, a smell, a perfume, we all know this, but it can be described as sweet or foul, heavy or slight, lasting or fading, titillating or repugnant, but all have one thing in common – without moisture there is nothing at all. Moisture, to some degree, is everywhere about us, in the air and forming part of almost every substance. Scent is retained by moisture and its lasting quality is not determined by the size or the nature of the substance imparting the smell, but by the length of time it takes for all the moisture to evaporate. Expensive perfume has a slow evaporating base and will still be detectable weeks later, whereas a cheap toilet water created from the same source will be gone in a short time.

You will have already realised that the main scent of interest to the Police Dog is that of Man. With that in mind, let us look at 'man-scent', understand what it consists of and how it is left behind as a track or trail for the dog to follow.

The effort of a living body provides waste material which is being continually shed and left behind as we go on our way. Some material is microscopic and others more readily visible, i.e. dandruff, hair and sweat. Exhaling air and sweating are a continuous bodily process, becoming more intensified under exertion. The definition of a 'track' in the dog world is a smell or series of smells left by the passage of something and, of course, the stronger the smell the easier it becomes to follow. The odour each individual exudes comprises many things and is as personal as a set of finger-prints.

INDIVIDUAL SCENT

For a dog to 'track' he has to distinguish between the scents left by different people. The elements that he identifies are as follows: –

Race It is believed that each race has a distinctive body odour, which has absolutely nothing to do with personal hygiene.

Sex Women smell different to men, it is biological fact.

Food We are what we eat. Your diet will quite often be revealed by the smell of your breath or sweat. Garlic can be detected, even by the human nose, some days after the meal.

Regional scent Different parts of the body have their own peculiar smell i.e. armpits, nape of the neck and feet to name but three.

These combine with ADITIONAL SCENT

Hygiene All manner of soaps, deodorants, anti-perspirants and perfumes are used, each with its own smell.

Clothing Wool, cotton, nylon, rayon and all other materials have their own distinctive smell which becomes heavily impregnated with the body smell of the wearer, together with any cleaning agents which have been used.

Footwear All types of footwear, as with clothes, have a smell of their own, together with personal foot odour combined with polish, creams etc. Most footwear is porous and acts almost like a sponge, sucking in and squeezing out odour as we walk.

Occupation When working in a heavily contaminated area, such as mechanics' workshop which abounds with oil, then the body and clothing become impregnated with the smell of oil.

When a person moves, not only does he start to lay a trail of scent on the ground but he also starts to form a tunnel of scent exuding from the body from head to toe, in the surrounding air. Movement also brings into force another factor, EARTH SCENT which comprises: –

Disturbed ground As we walk the ground beneath our feet is disturbed, tiny particles of soil, sand or grit are moved and are transferred from one place to another. Whenever this happens gasses and moisture, which have been trapped, escape. A stagnant pool gives an example of this action, detectable by our own noses. The pool before it is stepped in and the mud at the bottom disturbed, will have no detectable smell but afterwards a revolting stench will be released.

Bruised and crushed vegetation When any form of vegetation is trodden on the outer covering layer is broken and moisture released together with scent. New mown grass has a very strong smell and is another example that is quite easily detectable by the human nose.

We have examined what a trail of scent is made of, what we must now consider is what factors affect SCENT RETENTION.

Time combined with exposure For moisture to evaporate it must be exposed to the air. Any strong smelling liquid, if bottled, will retain its scent for as long as the bottle is corked, which can be hundreds of years. Time, by itself, does not destroy scent, only when combined with other factors which cause evaporation does time come into play. It is the rate of *evaporation* that directly affects the length of time scent can be detected. A rising temperature will increase the rate of dissipation and conversely a lowering temperature will reduce it.

Wind, both wet and dry, is a great enemy as it always disperses scent and makes it harder to follow. (This is only in relation to following a track. Wind does, however, make it easier if one is trying to locate a static source i.e. a hidden person.)

Although moisture is essential, too much as in the case of heavy rain will obliterate it. A light rain after a track has been laid can have the effect, especially on dry ground, of freshening the track and giving more scent to follow. A frost can have the effect of sealing the scent to the ground and only allowing it to be released at the time of a thaw, when of course other factors will start to work upon it.

We have all seen, on television or film, times when a person has evaded dogs by running along a stream or swimming across water. This evasion is a figment of the storytellers' imagination, for no greater assistance could be given than the fugitive getting wet. When entering the water one not only assists by disturbing the water-bed, still giving a scent to follow above the water, but also gives a far fresher track after leaving the water.

It must not be forgotten that, although the dog is the absolute master in the art of following a track, when a police team is in operation the handler also develops the art of field-craft. If the dog should lose the track, the handler can help find it again by for instance identifying a footprint or taking the dog to an area where he is most likely to regain the track.

I have, for many years, listened to tales of how tracking dogs could be thwarted, but they have invariably been from the kind of person who would be able to benefit from such intimate knowledge. Such things as pepper and aniseed sprinkled on the ground have been thought to throw a dog off the scent, and many a captured criminal has tried to lure an opinion from me on such substances, especially against their secret formula, 'which they forgot to bring'. These were attempts, no doubt, to get me to acknowledge that there was such a substance. "You've only caught me 'cause I forgot to bring it" has been the comment made by criminals after having been arrested at the end of a track. From my own experience, I can say there is nothing that will stop a good dog tracking.

Experiments carried out to negate the scent of a human

body or of clothing did not succeed because, although a man could be encased in a non-porous material, it did not exclude the elements of ground disturbance and exhaled breath. In 1926, Rowland Johns in his book *Let Dogs Delight* provides the only written record I can find of 'foiling the dogs':

> The astute criminal who fears being tracked by a police-dog is said to find that petrol is an excellent eradicator of scent and that he is fairly safe on a road much used by motor traffic. Continental criminals, in districts where police-dogs are much used, have now made a practice of carrying petrol with them whilst on their nefarious employment. This they sprinkle as they leave the scene of their crime.

I can, once more, say that after carrying out experiments this idea did not work and that if anyone did try it then the petrol can itself would provide excellent evidence to prove they were the person that had been tracked.

> The man who has conferred the greatest benefit upon the human race is the primitive savage who first tamed a litter of wolf cubs.
>
> SIR ROBERT BALL, LL.D., F.R.S.

Chapter 8

INCREDIBLE BUT TRUE: TRACKING STORIES FROM SOUTH AFRICA

While the use of police dogs in Great Britain was still a fledgling enterprise, in 1927 at Quaggapoort, near Pretoria, South Africa, a dog training camp was in full flourish. Thirteen trainers and 140 dogs in different stages of instruction were the nucleus for the whole country. The dogs in use were Airedale-Bloodhound cross, Dobermann Pinschers and the Airedale. Each handler qualified with two dogs under his charge before being passed out and posted to a district. With the reputation of having the ability to track a scent up to 72 hours old, these teams were called upon to travel some distances to the scene of a crime.

The following case histories, supplied in 1929 to The Police Journal by Colonel I.P. DeVilliers, MC, Commissioner, South African Police, are recorded as typical of the successes achieved.

During the night of 15th May 1927, a storeroom was broken into and foodstuffs stolen. A report to the Police Station was made at 9.30am the next morning and police dogs were requested. At 10.15pm, that night, two Dobermann Pinschers, Vrystaat and Vinjo, arrived at the scene with their handler. At 10.20pm, the dog Vinjo was put to track from a booted footprint at the scene, whereupon the dog followed the scent for a distance of 2½ miles, entered a native hut and barked. The hut was searched and the stolen goods found. A man was subsequently arrested, charged and sentenced to six months imprisonment with hard labour.

At 4.45pm on the 25th June 1927, a case of rape was reported to the police. The scene was visited and a footprint of the alleged offender found. On the strength of this police dogs were requested and arrived at the scene at 9am, 27th June (some 40 hours 15 minutes after the initial report). The dog Pauline (Dobermann Pinscher-Setter cross) tracked from the footprint for three miles to a hut, where she barked. The second dog, du Toit (Bloodhound-Airedale cross) was put to the same footprint as Pauline and followed the same trail, to the same hut, with the same result. As a result of this, and further enquiries, at 10pm the same day, a man was arrested and charged with the offence, after further evidence of identification by the complainant. He was subsequently found guilty and sentenced to 10 years imprisonment with hard labour.

[Although this story makes very good reading I find it hard to believe that evidence of the second track, as performed by du Toit, could be submitted. If the first track was truly accurate, then it would surely have been overlayed by the fresher and heavier scent of the handler and dog, Pauline.]

On the 7th August 1927 a case of sheep stealing occurred but it was not reported until 13th August, six days afterwards. A handler, with dogs Trix (Dobermann Pinscher) Rissikin (Bloodhound-Airedale cross), attended the scene and the dog Trix was put to track from a footprint, believed to be that of the offender. From 3.30pm, that day until the evening of the 14th August the dog continued to the point of exhaustion. At 4am, the next morning, the dog Rissikin was put to track from the spot where Trix had stopped. The dog continued the trail for a further 50 miles where he pointed out a man whose belongings were searched. Two sheepskins and fresh fat were found in his possession and as a result he was charged with stock theft and subsequently sentenced to two years' imprisonment with hard labour.

Part III

YOU AND YOUR DOG

Grooming session during a training course in the 1950s. PC Johnson (left) and PC Lloyd.

It is a strange destiny that dog has accomplished for himself. In the whole of illimitable space no other living thing loves man, believes in him, or unquestionably puts the power of life and death for himself in mans' hand.

BOOTH TARKINGTON

Chapter 9

THE LAW RELATING TO YOU
AND YOUR DOG

Every man has a right to keep even a fierce dog for the protection of his property against trespassers provided that this is a reasonable precaution in the circumstances.

This is a statement made in relation to the Guard Dog Act 1975. Laws govern society, providing rules for acceptable behaviour. Dogs, being part of the British way of life, have not been exempted from laws or civil actions against the owner or handler. It must be stressed that what follows is only a brief outline of the many and complex laws passed since 1847.

Purchasing A Dog
When purchasing a dog from someone 'in the trade', remember that they are governed by the Trade Description Act 1968. If there is any false description in relation to sex, breed or cross, fertility and soundness, there is power to take action and obtain a refund etc. If buying from a pet shop, ask if it is licensed under the Pet Animals Act 1951?

   Bear in mind! If anyone dealing with dogs does not comply with the law governing them, are they to be trusted?

   Breeders are governed by the law under the Breeding of Dogs Act 1973 which states: "It is an offence to keep a breeding establishment (which includes a private house) where more than two bitches are kept for the purposes of breeding for sale, without a licence by the Local Authority."

   When purchasing a dog from anyone, if a pedigree is given then it must be correct to the best of their knowledge and belief, otherwise it is quite possible offences of forgery and obtained money by deception might be taking place.

Gaining Ownership Of A Dog By Way Of Gift
If you are in public service beware: the Public Bodies

Corrupt Practices Act 1889, and the Prevention of Corruption Acts 1906 and 1916 all basically state that it is an offence to accept any gift which can be looked upon as an inducement or reward for giving favour.

Finding A Dog

When finding a dog you must report the 'finding' to the police, otherwise you could be guilty of theft under the Theft Act 1968, as a dog is classed as property. If the owner is unknown then you may keep the dog until such time as the owner makes claim.

Other laws may be classified into those which protect the dog from others, and those which protect others from the dog.

PROTECTION OF THE DOG

Protection of Animals Act 1911 – this Act creates offences by committing, or allowing the following to be committed:
1. Cruelly beating, kicking, ill-treating, torturing, infuriating or terrifying or by omitting to do any act which will cause any unnecessary suffering to any animal (this can include failing to provide food, water or veterinary attention).
2. Conveying or carrying on, in such a manner as to cause unnecessary suffering to any animal.
3. Causing, procuring or assisting at the fighting, or baiting of any animal or keeping, using, managing, or acting or assisting in the management of any premises or place for such purposes or the receiving of money for admission.
4. Wilfully, without reasonable cause or excuse administering any poisonous or injurous drug or substance to any animal.
5. Subjecting any animal to an operation which is performed without due care and humanity.

Under this Act the word 'cruelty' must be considered at all times during training when firm handling is required. Cruelty implies 'the infliction of unnecessary pain', therefore great care must always be taken. 'Unnecessary' comes into effect the very moment after you achieve the desired result, as in separating dogs that are fighting, or attempting to. To defend yourself from attack cannot amount to cruelty.

Abandonment of Animals Act 1960 – creates an offence to abandon a dog without reasonable cause or excuse, whether permanently or not, in circumstances likely to cause it unecessary suffering.

Veterinary Surgeons Act 1966 – creates an offence for any person, other than a qualified vet, to provide medical treatment to a dog except for emergency first aid.

Road Traffic Act 1972 – creates an offence of not keeping a dog on a lead, held by its handler, whilst on a road 'designated' by the Local Authority.

Dogs Act 1906 Amended 1988-90 – any dog which is unaccompanied in a public place may be detained by a Police Officer or Dog/Animal Warden for a period of seven days. During this time they must ensure that it is properly cared for and returned to the owner, if claimed. Dogs not claimed may be sold or destroyed in an approved manner.

Animal Health Act 1981 – All dogs must wear a collar and carry the name and address of the owner at all times when in a public place. There are exceptions to the rule which are sheep dogs whilst working, packs of hounds, dogs being used to destroy vermin and dogs taking part in a sporting event.

PROTECTION FROM THE DOG

Town Police Clauses Act 1847 – creates an offence for any person to suffer to be at large any un-muzzled ferocious dog or sets on or urges any dog to attack, worry or put in fear any person or animal. However, you may use your dog to assist you (as do Police Dog Handlers) under Section 3(1) of the Criminal Law Act 1967 where force is reasonable in the circumstances: –
1. In the prevention of crime
2. Effecting or assisting in the lawful arrest of an offender
   OR suspected offender
   OR of persons unlawfully at large

Dog Act 1897, Dangerous Dogs Act 1989, Dangerous Dogs Act 1991 – these Acts combine together to cover the subject of dogs which bite, attempt to bite or put people in fear, with the exception of Police Dogs and dogs of the armed forces.

Environmental Protection Act 1991 – creates offences of:
1. Keeping an animal in such a place or a manner as to be a nuisance or a danger to the public health.
2. Causing noise so as to be a nuisance or damage to public health, this includes the barking of a dog.
3. Allowing your dog to foul a public place.

Dogs Act 1906, Wildlife and Countryside Act 1981 – creates offences of a dog being allowed to harm protected species of wildlife and to chase, worry or kill livestock. Any dog found under such circumstances amongst livestock can be lawfully killed, providing the incident is reported to the police within 24 hours. This applies whether or not the handler is with the dog.

If you display a sign on your gate with the words *Beware of the dog, Enter at your peril, Make my day,* etc you are, in my opinion, already admitting you are the owner of a dangerous dog. Also these signs may admit liability to any damage the dog may do, even if it escapes through no fault of the owner/handler.

These signs do not exempt you from liability if the gate can be opened or a wall climbed over; who is to say that everyone can read, or if they can, that they believe what they read? There are those also who need to approach or enter premises to go about their lawful business for example, Police Officer, window cleaner or postman. All occupiers of premises must owe care to a visitor and under the Occupiers Liability Act 1957, the visitor must be left in no doubt as to what danger he faces if he fails to comply with the occupier's wishes, this may require a verbal warning and an acknowledgement of understanding. If a person ignores your warning, for example of a dog which is aggressive, and recklessly goes towards the dog then he may be regarded as being the author of his own misfortune.

The law of Trespass on land does not apply to dogs as it is accepted in law that there is a general difficulty in preventing them. However, there is liability if damage is caused.
Guard Dog Act 1975 – It is an offence to use or permit the use of a guard dog unless a handler capable of controlling the dog is present OR the dog is secured so that it cannot roam freely about the premises. Warning signs must also be displayed at each entrance to the premises where guard dogs are being used.

Having briefly acquainted yourself with these laws, you must have now realised that a well-behaved, well-trained dog is less likely to being discredit to you.

Chapter 10

YOUR DOG, YOUR CHOICE

Most people have already made their choice of dog before they seek advice and will not be swayed by anything adverse, however well-intentioned. You have your dog, whatever its breed, age and previous training. What I suggest that you ask yourself is, what are you trying to demand of this new addition to the family?

Let us first consider how the different breeds came about. It is a recognised fact that the dog evolved from the wolf and as long as 12,000 years ago, selective breeding had begun. From those times to the present day, quite distinctive breeds have been produced. Falling into 6 separate classes, as defined by the Kennel Clubs of the world, they are denoted by their primary use: –

Gun dogs Flushing game
Hounds Oldest known dogs – to track and run down game
Terriers Rodent exterminator
Toy dogs As their name suggests, a plaything
Utility dogs Used for unknown or obsolete purposes
Working dogs Guarding, shepherding etc.

The instinctive abilities for which these dogs were selected and bred is now, being steadily de-tuned by keeping the majority as household pets, although we are keeping the body shape.

The instinct of any breed should always be taken into consideration by the owner e.g. the Elkhound, bred to range out and away from its handler to locate its quarry, to bark and hold it at bay until the arrival of the handler, is by its very nature extremely vocal and headstrong. The Rhodesion Ridgeback, bred to run alongside horses and hunt lions. The Springer Spaniel, always on the move and ahead of the handler. These dogs and their like are naturally going to provide some difficulty to the handler where implicit, close to hand obedience is required.

Consider what the dog is capable of, before asking it to do too much. A limousine is not used for rallying and likewise a hot-rod is not used for state occasions. Hopefully you have made the right choice and a little training will provide the required results. If not, you may have to live with the unattainable for some years.

A cross-breed may give you any combination of the instinctive abilities.

Before giving a dog a permanent home, it is fair, both to the dog and yourself, to list what is acceptable behaviour in your dog and reject what is not. To bring a dog into your household without forethought can produce untold problems.

If you have chosen an adult dog, from a 'rescue centre' or otherwise, you will have now realised that you have inherited not only some good points but also every bad habit. Not knowing how these habits came about will make the re-training all the more difficult. The advice of an experienced trainer is required under these circumstances. Rarely can true remedial work be taken from the page of a book. Dog trainers can usually be found by consulting your local Police Dog Section or by asking your vet.

A rollicksome, frolicsome rare old cock
As ever did nothing was our dog Jock;
A gleesome, fleasome, affectionate beast,
As slow at a fight, as swift at a feast,
A wit among dogs, when his life 'gan fail,
When his years grew long and his eyes grew dim,
And his course of bark could not strengthen him.
Never more now shall our knees be pressed
By his dear old chops in their slobbery rest.
Nor our mirth be stirred at his solemn looks,
As wise, and as dull, as divinity books.
Our old friend's dead, but we all well know
He's gone to the Kennels where the good dogs go,
Where the cooks be not, but the beef bones be,
And his old head never need turn for a flea.

JAMES PAYN (1830-98)

Chapter 11

THE CARE OF YOUR DOG

Your dog cannot tell you when anything is wrong.

A healthy dog is a happy dog, is a good working dog and a willing pupil. To ensure that your dog is in continued good health a daily visual inspection is essential. This begins at first sight, in the morning, when the following should be borne in mind:

1. Is he his normal self (greeting behaviour – happy to see you etc.)?
2. Is he lethargic?
3. Is he limping?
4. Is there anything unusual about him, marks, lumps, bumps, movements etc?
5. Has he fouled?

Anything which is unusual should be noted as this can be of invaluable assistance to the Veterinary Surgeon, should his services be required.

If there is any fouling either from vomit or faeces these should be checked very carefully for abnormal signs (colour, consistency, presence of blood, mucus etc.) and foreign bodies (parasites, roundworm, tapeworm and other objects, plastic etc.).

Always take care to examine the first faeces of the day as this can give early signs of disease, intestinal problems or injury. Urine can also disclose abnormalities and note should also be taken.

If everything appears OK then the next important stage is a physical examination. To save the painful experience of bending for a lengthy time, a 'grooming block' can be a great help. Made from a log, or bricks, it should stand about 18in high and 12in square. With the dog standing, both forelegs on the block, a physical examination consists of checking the whole of the body; running your fingertips through the hair and over the skin will reveal any tenderness, lumps, injuries or foreign bodies. Next, pay special attention to the body orifices which are the ears, eyes, nostrils, mouth, penis/vulva and anus. Followed by feet, legs and scrotum.

Ears

Any reddening, swelling or large amounts of discharge are abnormal. A strong smell, shaking of the head, holding the head to one side, scratching or pawing at the ear, indicating pain when the ear is touched, show need for veterinary treatment. If the ears are dirty they can be cleansed with cotton wool and warm water, but take care not to probe any further than you can see. No oil or other medication should be poured into the ears without veterinary advice. I have detected ear mites by keeping the dog in complete darkness for a time, and then shining a torch into the ear. These almost microscopic parasites became visible on the ear flap before scurrying back into the ear canal.

Eyes

The eyes should be clear and bright and the surrounding membrane pink in colour. Any discharge, inflammation, discolouration or being bloodshot show the need for advice. Any discharge from the eyes can be lifted out with damp cotton wool and should not be merely rubbed away. The dog has a third eyelid (nictitating membrane) which is used to protect the eye in the same way as a human would use an eye patch. Any prominence of this eyelid can denote an eye injury.

Nose

This should be moist and cool, with no discharge. A hot and dry nose may denote a high temperature, but during hot weather or exercise, this can be the normal thing.

Mouth

An early indication of a stomach disorder, or worm infestation in the dog, is foul breath (any different from the norm!). Sore or cracked lips can be the reason why the dog shows a lack of enthusiasm in the retrieve exercise. A check should be made of the teeth for loose or broken ones, gum disease etc. Large marrow bones, given occasionally, will help to keep both teeth and gums in good condition.

Legs And Feet

Careful inspection of the legs and feet is important to detect signs of foreign bodies (thorns, grass seeds, glass, tar etc.)

Pads sometimes wear thin when the dog is not used to, or has had prolonged walking on, a hard surface such as concrete. However, dogs' feet do harden to such surfaces and the condition should not be too prolonged.

When dogs are kennelled, or generally in contact with hard surfaces, callouses may develop on the outer side of each foreleg, caused by laying on such a surface. This can be regarded as normal unless it becomes swollen or inflamed.

Genitals

The penis is located in a fold of skin known as the prepuce. There is often a slight discharge of a greenish-yellow matter, which the dog clears by itself. However, if this discharge is heavy and permanent (Balanitis) veterinary advice should be sought. Treatment is normally by the basic principle of cleanliness: bathing with a mild disinfectant and application of prescribed antibiotic ointment. The scrotum should be examined for any inflammation etc. Care must be taken when using strong bleach or disinfectant on floor areas as this can easily cause burns to exposed skin, such as the genital area.

The female genital tract, the vulva, should be free of discharge, apart from during Oestrus, or heat period.

Anus And Anal Glands

The anus should be clean and free from any reddening or soreness. On either side of the rectum, near the anus, are anal glands which sometimes become blocked, causing the area around the anus to become swollen and inflamed. A typical sign of this blockage is the dog trying to relieve itself by drawing its bottom along the ground in the sitting position. The evacuation of these blocked glands, I can assure you, is best left to the expert.

During general examination always keep a sharp eye open for parasites such as fleas, lice, ticks etc which can be easily treated.

Recognise the unusual — record it — seek advice.

GROOMING

Grooming, together with daily examination, good food, good housing and exercise is essential to keep the dog in good condition. A well-groomed dog looks good and brings credit to you. The full reasons for grooming are:

1. To massage the skin, which stimulates blood supply to the hair follicles and also activates the sebaceous glands to produce sebum and give a glossy coat.
2. To remove dead hair, dirt, scurf etc, thus helping prevent parasites and disease.
3. The physical contact between handler and dog helps cement the relationship between them.

The grooming method must be adopted to enable both dog and handler to get some pleasure from this proceedure. Comfort is of primary importance, especially for the handler's back! The dog can be raised either by putting it on a table or, with a larger dog by raising its front feet on a block. Both table and block must be firm and steady, with a non-slip surface, to promote confidence in the dog.

Grooming tools: Handler's hands, medium brush, comb, velvet, chamois leather or silk.

Hands Before using a brush or comb, the whole body of the dog should be given a vigorous massage with the hands and fingertips. This will initially loosen dead hair, stimulate the skin and also form part of the daily examination.

Brush A medium hard brush will be suitable for most breeds. A scrubbing motion, against the lay of the coat, will again stimulate the skin, remove dead hair, dirt, dried mud etc, and discourage parasites. During this time the brush can be dipped occasionally into a mild disinfectant which will also discourage parasites.

Comb Use of the comb should be minimal. A good steel comb with wide-set, smooth ended teeth should only be used to smooth the lay of the coat and disentangle hair. Great care should be taken not to pull out or damage live hair.

Velvet, Chamois Leather Or Silk This is the final spit and polish. These fabrics are ideal for final smoothing and bringing the shine to the dog's coat.

Hands Used once again, dipped in water and shaken dry, also form an ideal finish.

Hygiene

All faeces should be removed and disposed of. Nothing alienates people more than dog dirt lying around where it can be trodden in or where there are children playing. There is no need for the expense of special 'dog scoops', plastic bags are ideal. Use them like a glove, turn inside out and tie, then dispose of them.

Use disinfectant at the recommended level when appropriate. However, where there is a strong presence of urine, a weak dilution of household bleach is better (sometimes certain disinfectants react with urine to cause an even more unpleasant smell).

Food bowls and utensils should be kept clean and solely for use by the dog.

Grooming brushes, combs etc. should be kept clean and a separate kit used for each dog.

Always wash your hands after handling your dog.

Bathing

Most dogs hardly ever have a bath and appear none the worse for it. Dogs do not perspire through the skin and therefore any regular need for bathing is minimised. When a bath or shower *is* required don't use the garden hose, use lukewarm water and a proper dog shampoo. Rinse thoroughly and ensure that the dog is completely dry before being allowed out.

If bathing is impracticable, then a good way of removing dust from the dog's coat is to rub some talcum powder or fine dry sawdust into it, followed by an extensive grooming session.

Trimming And Stripping

This is best left to the professional, but no harm is done by generally keeping an eye on the places where discomfort can occur and clipping when necessary i.e. at the back of the ears where hair balls can form, and cutting long hair from between the toes (long hair can cause lameness if it becomes caked in mud, snow or ice).

FEEDING YOUR DOG

Food provides the necessary nutrients the dog requires to maintain the body, build new cells and tissues and the energy required in working muscles, breathing, digestion and keeping warm. Thus the amount of food required obviously depends on bodyweight, growth, living conditions and

workload. 'We are what we eat', looking at the constituent raw materials of the dog gives us a guide as to what should be fed. The raw materials of the average dogs are: –
56% Water
23% Fat
16% Protein
3½% Minerals
1½% Carbohydrate
The dog needs a daily input of all these to live, but not in the same proportions.

Carbohydrates are groups of carbon, hydrogen and oxygen, consisting mainly of sugars and starches which are digested to provide glucose. Although glucose can be extracted from proteins and fats it is far more readily available from carbohydrates, and in effect more cheaply fed. The normal source is biscuit, forming some 65% of the whole diet. Carbohydrates also contain fibre, which is indigestible and provides roughage for the digestive system.

Fats provide the body with its most concentrated form of energy, being twice the value of the same weight of carbohydrate or protein. Fats also have two other roles: they provide Essential Fatty Acids and carry fat-soluble vitamins. These Essential Fatty Acids cannot be manufactured by the dog's own body and thus must be fed as part of the diet. Dogs love fat and most prepared foods have coatings of it.
The recommended amount in the diet is 5%.

Proteins contain amino acids which are used to replace dead and repair damaged cells. They can also be utilised for energy. They should form at least 13% of the whole diet. It is the quality of protein, which is important. Meat is high in protein and is far more digestible than protein derived from cereals, for instance, which is only 50% digestible whereas an egg is 95% digestible.

Vitamins play an important part in regulating a dog's metabolism. They are neccessary for normal health and bodily functions. A dog's body can manufacture vitamins C and D but all other vitamins have to be absorbed from the diet. Vitamins A, D, E, and K can be stored in body fat, but B complex vitamins have to be supplied daily, these are water soluble and any excess cannot be stored in the body. Any good quality commercial dog food will include B vitamins.

Minerals such as calcium and phosphorous are used for growth and repair. Other minerals are used in enzymes and proteins and help control the body fluid balance.

Vitamins as well as minerals if fed in excess, normally by way of supplements, can cause abnormalities in growth and may in fact be poisonous.

Fresh water may not be a nutrient, but it is a vital part of the diet. The dog can survive far longer without food than it can without water. As previously stated, it forms 56% of the dog's body. Water fulfils many roles, including being a solvent and the principal constituent of blood.

The Types Of Food Available

There are many ways to provide the nutrients a dog needs to stay healthy. Other aspects to consider include – cost, availability, convenience and palatability. To prepare a satisfactory diet completely from fresh foods requires skill. It is impossible without proper analysis to estimate accurately the protein and fat content of a piece of meat. Meat has to be cooked to kill any bacteria or parasites present, but over-cooking will reduce its food value. Vegetable content is also hard to provide whilst giving palatability.

The most practical and modern way is to feed commercially prepared pet foods which can be found in three basic types – canned foods, semi-moist foods and dry foods.

Canned foods are very popular because they are convenient, easy to store and very palatable to the dog. They contain all the necessary nutrients, but are low in terms of energy content. Most canned foods are classed as 'complementary' (as opposed to being a complete food) and are meant to be fed in combination with other foods, particularly biscuits which provide the main energy or carbohydrate supply of the diet.

A typical analysis of a canned food is 9% protein, 5% fat, 1.5% carbohydrate and a staggering 70-80% water.

Semi-moist foods are normally contained in a sausage-type packaging, they usually have a long shelf life and appeal to owners who prefer convenience as an alternative to feeding fresh meat. They contain all the necessary nutrients and have a good energy value, therefore not requiring as much biscuit as tinned foods.

A typical analysis of a semi-moist food is 19% protein, 10% fat, 38% carbohydrate and 26% water.

Dry foods are a complete food, requiring no further addition to the diet. They are usually made up from concentrated animal protein, cereals, fats and have added mineral and vitamin supplements. These foods contain a higher concentration of nutrients than other prepared foods and it is, therefore, quite easy to overfeed if the manufacturers recommendations are NOT complied with.

A typical analysis of this type of food is 22% protein, 7% fat, 51% carbohydrate and 15% water.

So, it is completely up to you what you feed, just as long as it is a well-balanced diet. The general health and condition of your dog will quickly reflect this.

When To Feed Your Dog

The practicalities of feeding your dog are directly related to your family group. Aiming for a regular feeding time may be impossible due to working shifts. Most dogs are fed one meal a day, but others may require a number of separate smaller meals to aid proper digestion. Deciding the time of day to feed is up to you, however, time must always be allowed after a meal for the dog to be given light exercise in order to evacuate himself. Shutting a dog away with a full stomach and bladder is asking for trouble.

My own dogs are given twenty minutes within which to eat their meal. Anything left after that time is thrown away. If food is left out, particularly the moist type, it will attract flies and go stale, promoting disease.

If there is any noticeable decline in food intake, as with any other abnormality, then veterinary advice should be sought.

Chapter 12

COMMON HEALTH PROBLEMS

Sickness and Diarrhoea

Sickness and diarrhoea are the symptoms of many diseases, all of which my dogs are vaccinated against. However the most common cause is gastro enteritis, which arises as follows: – the bacteria which are normally present in the bowel cause no problems unless the bowel is stressed, when the environment becomes more favourable to their growth and then numbers increase sharply, causing inflamation and damage to the linings of the stomach and intestines. The following is a list of common stresses:

Change of diet
Change of water supply
Change of home circumstances i.e. kennelling
Change of routine
Change of climate conditions
Travelling
Excitement in working or play.

Occasional vomitting is a natural action of the dog and can be done at will. The dog will resort to this in the event of a ticklish throat or upset stomach, normally eating grass first to provide a binding agent. Gastro enteritis should clear within two days, during which it is acceptable to starve the dog but always keep fresh water available (vomitting and diarrhoea will dehydrate the body).

Kennel Cough

A cough, once again is a symptom of various other diseases. Kennel cough is usually associated with boarding kennels and has a variety of causes, all of which produce a harsh, dry, hacking cough but usually the dog remains bright and alert. If left untreated the disease can spread down the respiratory tract and cause pneumonia. It is highly contagious and any dog suspected of having the disease should be isolated immediately. As an initial treatment a childs cough medicine bought from any chemist can be used to alleviate the cough, but a vet should always be consulted at the earliest opportunity.

Worms

Worms are present in all dogs, whether as adults or eggs in the lungs or digestive tract, or larvae in the tissues. It is impossible to rid the body of them completely. There are two main types of worms which affect dogs in Britain: roundworms and tapeworms. The most common is the roundworm or *Toxocara Canis,* in adult form it is between 1½in and 4in long, looking like cooked spaghetti.

The bitch passes on larvae to her unborn puppies in the womb and by the time the pups are born adult reproductive worms are present. However some larvae will remain within a bitch puppy's tissues until her first pregnancy when they will be passed on to *her* unborn puppies. Eggs are passed out by faeces and it is by this manner they can infect other animals, including humans. Worming tablets can be obtained from a pet shop or vet and used to rid the dog of adult worms, thus greatly reducing the risk to other animals. Adopt a regular worming programme.

The easiest way to detect worm infestation is to examine faeces. In the case of roundworm, they can be seen live and wriggling. Examine any mucus passed, as smaller worms can be seen, best described as swimming. Revolting to look at, they must be cleared away as soon as possible and the area disinfected.

Once with Ryan, I found what appeared to be a piece of bone in his faeces. It was small, white and square. Prodding it with a stick, it moved, it was alive! Treating the dog with worming tablets, some hours later Ryan was seen, showing some discomfort, with a tapeworm hanging from his backside, intact. Eventually the worm was ejected and I collected it up in a plastic bag. Taken to the vet, it was washed, still quite alive and some 6 feet in length. The drugs given had merely stunned the worm, allowing it to be passed. This particular worm was subsequently place in formalin and kept as a bottled specimen. Ryan had shown no ill effects whilst harbouring this parasite and its detection was due to the daily routine.

Blocked Anal Glands

The dog has two anal glands, one at each side of the anus, approximately at the 4 and 8 o'clock positions. These are modified skin glands which produce a secretion to lubricate the passage of a motion, and they are also scent glands. The glands are liable to become blocked, particularly in German Shepherd dogs, probably because of the down-pressed tail carriage. When this occurs there is quite a lot of irritation and the dog will rub its bottom, look round at its tail, or lick and bite at the tail root. Normal treatment is to squeeze the glands and empty the sacs but I would recommend this is done by a vet. A most foul smelling fluid is exuded and will almost certainly require the destruction of any clothing it is deposited on. A job definitely not for the amateur!

Assisting The Vet

In all cases of illness I recommend that a Veterinary be consulted. Whenever you take your dog to the vet, the first question is, normally, "What's wrong with him?" A dog cannot speak for himself and, unless the reason is blatantly obvious such as a wound or limp, you will be required to give a full explanation. A precise outline will assist an early diagnosis. All abnormalities, of whatever description, including the date and time should have been noted. The vet should be made aware of your own suspicions. Anything, however simple, may form part of the pattern for diagnosis.

If your dog is ill-tempered or in pain, your ability to lift and control your dog is paramount. Your position, at the 'sharp end' is always most desirable as vets are just as prone to being bitten as anyone else.

Do not ask others to take the dog to the vet for you, they will not have your intimate knowlege if questioned.

Part V

TRAINING YOUR DOG

Man is the god of the dog; he knows no other; he can understand no other. And see how he worships him! with what reverence he crouches at his feet! with what love he fawns upon him! with what dependence he looks up to him! and what cheerful alacrity he obeys him! His whole soul is wrapt up in his god! all the powers and faculties of his nature are devoted to his service! and these powers and faculties are ennobled by the intercourse. Divines tell us that it just ought to be so with the Christian − but the dog puts the Christian to shame.

ROBERT BURNS (1759 – 96)

Chapter 13

ABOUT TRAINING

One of the greatest pleasures of owning a dog is for it to be obedient and in order to achieve this, training must be given.

The art of training is to fully understand the exercise yourself and then impart this knowledge to your dog. Basic requirements are a commonsense attitude, patience and a dog which is intelligent and willing to learn. Dogs, like humans, vary in ability and intelligence. The older one is, the harder it is to learn and so it is with the dog. However, care should be taken not to start extensive training too early, allow your puppy to grow and qualify in the 'University of Life' before being restricted by schooling.

Whilst contemplating a certain exercise, look at what you want the dog to do and why. It is pointless teaching something potentially hazardous when there is no positive use for it. Why teach your dog to jump when his only obstacle is your own garden fence, or teach him to tug on a rag which results in him bringing down the washing? Always look for a reason, should the dog ever steadfastly refuse. I have, on numerous occasions, experienced the initial refusal by the dog to retrieve metal. Hold anything metal in your own mouth and its taste, and hardness in contact with your teeth, will soon give you the reason for this objection.

All training is based on association and habit, make it easy for the dog to gain achievement and reward. He is not capable of backward or forward thinking and this, above all, must be remembered.

To start any exercise both dog and handler must be in a happy frame of mind and free from influences which might affect concentration. First and foremost, the dog must have been well walked and allowed to 'empty' for who can think or even walk straight with a full bladder. We all know that when sad or angry concentration becomes an effort, you have to enjoy what you are doing in order to give it your best. This also applies to the dog, he suffers the same states of mind, including stress. Other influences can consist of other dogs being trained at the same time, other members of the family in close proximity, loud noises etc.

Once an exercise has been learned, then outside influences can be steadily introduced as part of the programme. Smartness and attention to detail, whilst carrying out exercises, will give a polished performance by the dog. The old saying 'look at the dog and see the handler' becomes quite true. Your attitude plays a great part, the more relaxed you are the more relaxed your dog will be.

Commands should be given in different tones of voice according to the exercise; it is no good using a harsh voice when practising the recall, as this will cause the dog to stay away, or using a soft voice when he is misbehaving.

The same command should always be used for a particular exercise, given in the correct tone and always singularly; the command 'sit' for example, if used in quick succession will become 'sit, sit' and the dog will only respond after the second 'sit'.

The dog has a greater sense of hearing than our own and, unless he is some distance away, there is absolutely no reason to shout.

Continually nagging at the dog or jerking the lead and not correcting him properly will ultimately bore him, so making him disinterested. Constant repetition of the same exercise will give the same end result, especially if it was completed satisfactorily in the first instance. Variation, as they say, is the spice of life so a little training given often, combined with sufficient play to enable the dog to enjoy working, will give excellent results.

All types of training are forms of compulsion, however subtle, and with this in mind, it must be realised that when rewarded with sufficient praise, or the occasional tit-bit, the dog will be only too willing to comply with your wishes. During training the dog may sometimes become confused and it is at this point things invariably go horribly wrong. He may show his confusion in a variety of ways i.e. standing still not wishing to move, going into the down position or even running away. To become short-tempered will only increase the confusion and make matters worse. To overcome this obstacle, break off and get the dog to achieve a simple unrelated exercise, giving plenty of praise, and re-introduce the problem exercise later, using a different approach. Using the same approach will only invite the same result as before.

As an example of dogs' thinking ability, I have seen them freeze when asked to perform heelwork whilst carrying an object. Although the dog was able to do both exercises perfectly, separately, the moment they were combined led to confusion.

The limited reasoning power of the dog should always be borne in mind when any form of correction is required. He will only appreciate the correction or reward for what he has done at that very moment. How many times have you heard: 'And that's for not coming back straight away', the dog getting a smack for supposedly not returning when he is, in fact, sitting at the handler's side. No wonder he does not eagerly return the next time.

Any form of correction should be done verbally, if at all possible, using the word "NO", at the very moment of the wrongdoing. Any physical correction will lead to the dog shying away every time there is any sudden movement, thus making training more difficult.

Having gained all knowledge of the exercise from the handler, any fault that develops must lie with the method of training. It does no harm, even with an experienced dog, to revert to simple basics, effectively re-defining the exercise.

Should frustration or anger set in during any training, then the lesson is best ended there and then and concluded with throwing of a ball, or having a play to break the situation. If not, the dog will conclude, 'You don't like training, I am certainly beginning not to like it, what the hell are we doing here?'.

Initially, training should be carried out using a long lead in order that the dog be under proper control at all times.

Further Training Hints
1. Good training is based on mutual trust and the development of a bond between you and your dog.
2. Never scold the dog without good reason.
3. Remember, a dog cannot ask questions.
4. Be decisive, firm, know exactly what you want and how it should be done.
5. Never allow mistakes to occur, rectify them immediately if they do.
6. Reward everything that is done well.
7. The lead should be used to 'check' and not punish disobedience.
8. Success in training depends upon the ability of the handler to make the dog understand what he wants and then, by

repetition, make it almost instinctive.

9. The more a dog is taught, the easier it becomes to teach.

Training Commands

Remember, a dog cannot speak. A verbal command with immediate positive action, followed by reward or disapproval, is how a dog learns the meaning. The commands have to be given precisely and in the same tone of voice each time. The dog will only respond to one command at a time, invariably the last. He is incapable of understanding two or three commands when put together. The least number of commands in the 'training dictionary', will make it easier for both dog and handler to learn.

The following are the commands most commonly used:

Word and manner of tone	Desired result
HEEL short, sharp, firm	Be at my left side and follow me wherever I go.
COME light, friendly manner	Return to me directly.
STAND drawn out, soft	Stand and remain standing until further command.
SIT short, sharp, firm	Sit and remain sitting until further command.
DOWN short, sharp, harsh	Down and remain down until further command.
AWAY light	Go away from me, at a fast pace, in a straight line until further command.
FETCH light	Seek out, recover and return object to hand.
LEAVE firm	Give up, to hand, any object being held.
NO short, sharp, harsh	The admonitory command.
SPEAK light, sharp	Give voice, bark.
FINISH short, harsh	Cease barking.
FREE light, friendly	Release from command – playtime!

Care should be taken at all times when conversing with your dog so as not to include a 'command word' when the trained response is not required. If such a word is included, without realising, and the dog fails to respond immediately then you are actively de-training and allowing him to be disobedient.

You as a handler will quickly learn, that once your dog understands the single verbal command, there will be no need for other commands so often used to complement the first, i.e. if you dog understands the command HEEL there should be no need for other commands such as CLOSE, LEFT, RIGHT, ABOUT and so on. These extra commands satisfy our own needs but only suffice to confuse the dog.

As you may have already noticed, omitted from the list of commands are those of STAY and WAIT. These commands are two of the most common in use, but I ask, is there a need? By telling the dog to STAY or WAIT you will undoubtedly be combining it with the SIT, STAND or DOWN position, thereby giving the dog something extra to think about and understand. As a further example, when leaving the dog in the sit position, there is no need for 'stepping off' with the alternative foot, a flat hand in front of his face and another command of wait or stay. The dog is in the SIT position and should remain so until given another command.

Remember, the use of your dog's name will always provoke a response from the dog, invariably movement at a point when you least want it, so always think what you are saying. Always bear in mind:
· Things you can explain to a dog, by word of mouth, are very limited.
· The dog judges more by tone and expression than by the actual word spoken.
· The dog has a very simple and trusting mind and can only assimilate a little at a time.
· The simpler and more explicit the method, the better.

Finishing An Exercise
Before carrying out any training exercise, you must know how to let the dog know he is no longer under any compulsion. Therefore, at the end of each exercise if you go through the same proceedure, giving the same command, the dog is left in no doubt he has finished. My own procedure is command the dog to go to my left or 'heel' side, and ensuring the dog is in one of the discipline positions: Sit, Stand or Down, rub the dogs' chest with the right hand and then give the command FREE, accompanied with play and praise.

Admonishment

In many an old dog trainer's repertoire was the adage:

> A woman, a spaniel, and a walnut tree;
> The more you bash 'em, the better they be.

This will, of course, bring about a degree of compliance but it will always be under fear and stress. A happy working environment produces better results! The only time I advocate direct corporal punishment is if the dog, for some reason, attacks the handler and under these circumstances the dog can *never* be allowed to win.

A dog, at times, whether in training or otherwise will need to know he is doing something wrong. The application of direct punishment before the dog is being wilfully disobedient is both cruel and thoughtless. To whip a dog across the backside each time the dog goes in front, will not teach it to walk happily at heel but will cause it to hang back fearful and cringing.

A verbal reprimand of NO at the very moment the dog starts to do something wrong will distract him away from it, follow this with praise and you should achieve the desired result. If the dog does continue after this i.e. chewing at something undesirable, he will have undoubtedly moved his head to avoid eye contact, 'if he can't see you, you are not there'. If the dog is within reach, then a quick grab and shake of the scruff of the neck, again with a NO will have salutary effect. If you are a short distance away and have a good aim, a thrown check chain, with a sharp NO as it strikes his backside will have a startling effect. The dog will look up at you with an expression that seems to say: "Where the hell did that come from" and if you greet the dog with open hands, "I don't know, it must have been my voice", he will quickly learn.

Never make threats, always be in a position to carry out corrective measures, otherwise you will become totally ineffective to the dog and lose your role as teacher and leader.

Chapter 14

THE TRAINING EXERCISES

Heelwork

This is the worst exercise ever carried out by the average person. My experience is that most people first attend dog training classes to be able to take the dog for a walk on the lead, without having their arm pulled from its socket.

The first mistake is to use the wrong equipment. A short lead gives no room for correction and is forever taut, from the hand to the dogs' collar. The ideal length is about 6 feet, which can be shortened by clips, when necessary. A soft leather is better for the hands, as I have seen pain and blisters caused by both chain and flat nylon. An ordinary collar is all that is needed for the responsive dog, but for the strong and headstrong a slip collar or check chain may be necessary. Any form of check chain must be fitted correctly to ensure that whenever pressure is applied, the chain slackens as the pressure is released. Ask your supplier for a demonstration.

When using a check chain the ideal length is one that slips just over the head. The size of link should be relative to the length of hair, the longer the hair the larger the link. Using a small link on long hair causes it to become shorn around the neck and unsightly.

When walking with the dog on a lead, the dog should be by the left side, the lead held in the right hand with the left hand free. The lead should be slack, merely connecting handler to dog, not a means for pulling or being pulled. The reason for the dog being on the left side is simply to provide some uniformity. If the dog knows his position, then he will readily adopt that position at all times. It is also convenient for those who are right-handed, when using the lead as a training aid. The left side also provides conformity when entering tests and competitions. However, I believe that no-one should be precluded from any test or training, if their preferred position is for the dog to be on the right, providing they always stick to it.

The collar, of whatever description, should be worn high on the neck, beneath the chin and behind the ears and tight but comfortable. This gives the ultimate control as the collar is now at the weakest point of the neck and the slightest pressure will provoke an immediate response.

To prepare the dog for the heelwork exercise you must begin with the dog being under control from the start, and the ideal manner is for the dog to be in the SIT position, by the handler's left side, at the 'heel' position. When the dog is steady, the command HEEL should be given as the handler steps smartly forward. If you use a sharp, brisk pace the dog will respond better as this will be more towards his normal gait, especially a large dog. It must be borne in mind, from the very start that it is the handler who dictates the pace and direction, not the dog.

Repeating the command HEEL whilst on the move, the dog must be encouraged to keep close to the handler's left side. This can be done initially by clicking the fingers, patting the left thigh, fussing the dogs head and generally talking to him. If the dog is keen and excited by the whole episode and in his eagerness is jumping up and playful, this must not be discouraged at this time. Heelwork should be looked upon as a happy and cheerful exercise, too much control too early will only succeed in the dog disliking these lessons and he will forever work with a dejected look.

For the dog that is hanging back, lots of praise and encouragement are a must. If the dog is unresponsive to this then a morsel of food may provide the incentive required. I have known chocolate to be rubbed into the palm of the left hand to achieve this. Likewise a playtoy concealed in the left hand, with the rewards being given at the end of the exercise. I am in agreement with any incentive of this type being used so long as it is only used occasionally once the desired result has been achieved on a regular basis. Otherwise the exercise will be lost and the dog will only 'perform' when he has certain knowledge of that reward being available. All rewards should eventually be reduced to verbal or physical praise. The dog should never be dragged to heel.

If the dog is headstrong and will not respond to either praise or food, then physical correction is the order of the day. With the use of a 'check chain' collar, whenever the dog pulls in front then give a sharp upwards and sideways check with the lead, combined with the command HEEL. This should give the shock required to bring him back. Take care in not prolonging the 'check' and so making it a 'pull';

pressure should be released immediately the collar tightens on the neck, with immediate praise once the dog is back in position.

If the dog is still headstrong and not learning very quickly, then another approach is to make the dog very wary of your footsteps. Each time the dog makes to go in front then make a sharp turn to the left, effectively walking into the dog, this will make him start and have one eye on you all the time. This can, however, make the dog walk wide of you, to avoid this, find a long wall or fence and walk alongside with the dog between you and the barrier. Give plenty of fuss and praise whilst walking, each time the dog makes to go in front give the command HEEL and almost squeeze the dog back into position by walking close to the barrier.

The Recall

This exercise is where the dog is trained to return to the handler, upon command, ignoring any attractions or distractions.

If handling a very young puppy, the training may not require anything more than calling the dogs' name, accompanied by the command COME. Kneel or crouch down, with outstretched arms and give plenty of encouragement, together with much fuss and praise as the pup reaches you, it will quickly learn that this is one of life's most pleasurable things. To let the pup run away and play after this exercise, with no other formality, will assist training in the future. If the pup always associates the recall with the end of playtime, being put on the lead and taken home, it may well start to resist. Even though the pup may start to respond purely on its name being called, it is advisable to continue with the command, to lay down the basics for the future.

Problems occur when training starts late and the pup has been allowed to have its own way for some time. Nothing is more exasperating than shouting after a dog which is taking no notice whatsoever. Once the command has been given, the dog should on no account be allowed to disobey. If this happens then you are actively detraining the dog, teaching it that it is all right to do wrong. To chase after a dog that is ignoring a command will only provoke your wrath and give the impression of a wonderful 'chasing game'.

The recall is the hardest exercise to enforce and the only manner in which this can be done effectively is for a line (ideally a rope-type washing line) some 20 yards long to be attached to the dog's collar.

The Recall.

With the line attached, the dog should be allowed to go and play. When the dog is used to the free trailing line and his attention diverted, then is the time to pick up the line, give the dog's' name with the command COME. If the dog fails to respond immediately then a further command, combined with a sharp tug on the line and the action of 'hauling the dog in' will bring him in the required direction. With continued light commands and praise, the dog should eventually start to respond. As this happens the line should be slackened with more praise and fuss given. As with the pup, do not allow the dog to associate this exercise with the ending of further enjoyment.

If the dog is one of those that does not readily respond to fuss and praise then it is quite acceptable to use a morsel of food as a reward.

This lesson must be repeated consistently until the dog is responding without a second thought. It may take weeks before you can finish with the line. If the line is taken off too early the dog quickly realises that all control has gone with it, thus breaking the spell. Re-fitting the line after this failure will then only teach the dog to respond to the line and no progress will have been made.

If the dog is slow returning, but is not being disobedient, then the handler should turn and run away immediately after calling the dog, this will excite the fear of being left behind and cause him to run to you. Turn and face the dog as he reaches you to properly complete the exercise.

A game can be made of the recall by shouting the dog's name and then running away and hiding. This will, at first, prove to be somewhat nerve shattering for the dog, but the subsequent finding of his handler will give such relief and excitement that after a few lessons of this kind it will be difficult to give the dog the slip.

Bark or Speak, On Command
This exercise can take minutes or months to train, a lot depends upon the dog's temperament. The idea is to agitate the dog into some form of vocal response and then to reward it immediately. The easiest method is to have a play object, squeaky toy, ball etc, or a morsel of food in the hand and tease the dog with it. The moment the dog gives any whine or bark then the object is given or thrown for him. The dog will quickly realise the essence of the game when the 'tease' is combined with the command SPEAK.

In the beginning this command should be given frequently in a sharp and excited tone until the dog barks readily. Once this has been achieved, then you will have realised that once the dog has his reward in his mouth then the barking stops. Therefore what was initially the reward for barking can become the reward for being quiet. Thus, once the dog is barking upon the command SPEAK then with a firm command of FINISH and the reward presented to the dog, not thrown, the full exercise will have been achieved. By hiding the play object in a clenched fist and half raising the arm, combined with the command and only producing it at the bark, then one is on the way to the silent signal, when required.

If the dog continues to be dumb after some time using this method, then the partnership of a dog already performing the exercise may provoke the response when both are teased and commanded together. If that fails then use the excitment of 'feeding time', and do not place the food on the floor until a bark has ensued.

A trick I have often used to amuse school children is to ask the dog to do basic arithmetic. This is quite easy with a dog that gives a steady rythmic bark. By reducing the command to a mere hand signal i.e. pointing the finger, one can then ask the question, "What is 3 + 2?" whilst pointing, and then give a quick rub of the head after 5 barks, and "What a clever dog", astounds the audience. The rub of the dog's head being both the reward and the 'finishing' signal to the dog.

The Sit.

The Stand, The Sit, The Down

Why teach the dog to STAND? One simple reason is to keep the dog from getting dirty on a rainy day. Whilst walking with the dog on a lead he can be kept upright, on all fours. Another is when visiting the vet, it keeps the dog in the ideal position for taking his temperature. To name but two!

This exercise is first taught whilst walking with the dog on the lead. When coming to a halt, the command STAND is given in a long drawn out soft tone and at the same time gently caressing the dog's left flank with the left hand. If the dog starts to sag, it should never be lifted by the tail or forced roughly into position but gently lifted, again given the command and caressing motion.

Once the dog has learned the position then it can be re-enforced by keeping hold of the lead walking around the dog, in a circle, ever increasing in size until the lead can be dropped and eventually dispensed with. The SIT is a simple exercise whereby movement of the dog can be controlled and discipline instilled.

Once more, with the dog on the lead, if the dog sits naturally when you are standing then all that is needed is the command SIT as it sits and at any time should it start to move.

If the dog remains standing then lift the lead with the right hand above the dog's head and press the left hand on its rump, then the dog should sit. If the dog still resists, a sharp

The Down.

tap of the hand again on the rump should produce the desired result.

If, once again, the dog still resists then run the palm of the left hand, with fingers and thumb outstretched, down the backbone to a point just in front of the hips and give a squeeze, using the thumb and second finger, the dog will sit as if 'tickled' into position. Don't forget to give the command SIT as you do it. Holding a morsel of food above the dog's head will also bring this about very easily. But this method should be discontinued once the dog is responding to the verbal or hand signal.

The DOWN, in my opinion, is a life-saving exercise as well as being the most disciplinary. It is said that once a dog will lay down and stop down, on command, you have entered your dog's mind and training from then on will become a lot easier. In my own experience I have found this to be true.

Time and patience are paramount. As with all exercises, any temptation to hurry will bring about unreliability, but more so in this case. If the dog realises that the distance between you, or when you go out of sight, breaks the element of control then that control may be lost forever.

The exercise is mainly used when you wish to leave the dog but are unable to tie it up, or to make it drop into the DOWN position if any danger is forseen i.e. running into the path of a moving vehicle.

Before you can contemplate the down position, the dog must be confident about remaining in one place if you are to leave him. The only way is to tie the dog to something, but it must be remembered that when doing this the lead must be in an upward direction from the neck, otherwise the dog could become entangled in such a way as to cause harm.

When the dog is tied, without placing him in any position, giving a command, or fuss or anything else, just walk away a short distance. If you make a fuss or try to reassure the dog before leaving, then it will make the act of parting all the more heartbreaking to the dog. Having walked away a short distance, the idea is then to occupy yourself with some mundane task, not related to the dog, i.e. reading a book or newspaper. If the dog starts to make a fuss by barking, howling etc, take no notice whatsoever. If you so much as look or say something the dog will realise he has got your attention and so will create all the more when you turn away again. Once the dog settles, and it may take some time, then is the time to go to him and make a fuss. Complete the exercise at this point. Only when the dog is settled when you first leave him do you prolong the exercise by returning, giving a little praise and then leaving again.

The act of placing the dog in the down position invariably causes all the problems. A dog will lie out in the garden for hours on end, but the moment you wish him to lie down will be the time he resists.

With the lead attached to the dog's collar, and the dog at your left side, take hold of the lead with the right hand, then with the left hand grasp the end of the lead where it connects with the collar. With the command of DOWN, push hard with the left hand, taking the dog's head to the floor. If the dog resists violently then discontinue. However, if the dog's whole body follows and he becomes prone, immediately take the pressure away. If the dog then starts to rise, re-assert the pressure, but only until he is once again prone. These actions may continue a number of times before the dog accepts the situation. Your patience and perseverence will be on test! If you give up before achieving the desired result, then as in many other cases, you will have taught the dog that he is stronger and disobedience wins.

If the dog violently resists pressure to the neck, then the following should be adopted. Place the dog in the sit position and with the command of DOWN lift both front feet, using the right hand, with an upward and forward motion. Using the left hand to steady the shoulders continue until the desired position is reached. With a large dog place the right forearm behind the dog's right leg and grasp the dog's left pastern (wrist). As before, give the command DOWN and with an upward and forward motion place the dog in position.

If the dog resists this method then rather than using a lift and forward action, use a lift and sideways pull. The left hand pushing against the right shoulder, from the side and with the left leg pulled underneath its body the dog should go over onto its left side. Once the dog is in position then all pressure should be relaxed unless he attempts to move, then it should be re-asserted, using the DOWN command.

Once the dog is reacting to the command, readily and quickly, it can be tested (this can also apply to the SIT and STAND positions). The way to do this is whilst the dog is in position, give a gentle pull on the lead. If the dog reacts to the pull by moving in that direction give a further command whilst still applying tension. If the dog reacts by pulling back, straining against the tension and remaining in position, he has learned the command.

Now is the time to train the extension of the command i.e. not to move, whatever happens, until commanded to do something else ('whatever happens' should never include a life threatening situation when you are not in overall control). The extension means leaving the dog, in a commanded position, going some distance from him, including out of sight. Only under supervised test conditions do I advocate leaving a dog out of sight of its handler. Without supervision, a totally unforeseen situation could occur and I do not believe a dog should be put under such pressure.

Now that the dog suffers no anxiety when left, he should be placed in the down position, using the DOWN command, with the collar and lead still attached. Looping the lead over the dog's back, to give the dog a feeling of some physical control, leave the dog a short distance. If the dog starts to move then re-enforce with a further command of DOWN.

The dog should be relaxed when left and combined with the down position he should be comfortable and the distance and time for the exercise can be increased. This increase should be done in very slow stages so as not to cause alarm. Once the dog is performing the exercise well, the lead can be dispensed with.

Now the dog understands the command, include a DOWN whilst performing heelwork or when the dog is running free. The dog should drop immediately but if he does not then go towards him with 'scolding' tones and repeat the command. Once the dog goes down then walk away from him, returning to finish the exercise as outlined later. If there is ever need for the use of this command from a distance, do not use the dog's name as this will make him come to you, simply shout the command.

When *returning* to the dog, return to the heel side and stand for a few seconds before kneeling and giving praise. By doing this it will stop the dog anticipating the finish by rising or creeping towards you.

The Retrieve

Before contemplating teaching the retrieve exercise it is necessary that the dog be already proficient in the recall exercise.

The retrieve is one of the hardest exercises to teach if the dog does not take to it naturally. It should be instinctive for the dog to chase and play with any object thrown for him and then with the benefit of an already trained recall, for the dog to bring the object back to you and with a little more training for him to deliver it to hand.

Sounds simple! but what a hard job we make of it. Nearly everyone starts by throwing the article, sending the dog in pursuit and then trying every trick in the book to get him to bring it back. The dog has won his prize and not having been taught the 'exercise', will invariably hang on to it and induce a game of 'take it from me if you can'. The first objective is for the dog to hold any article given to him. Nothing should be thrust into the dog's mouth, but offered to him for him to take. Therefore the article used in the beginning should be something the dog is familiar with and which causes no discomfort to the mouth. As you are already aware, I do not believe in too many commands and therefore I do not include the word 'hold' at this stage. Eventually the command FETCH will in itself mean seek out, recover and return to hand, carry and hold it, do not drop.

The article should be easy to grasp and not promote any chewing action. My own preference is an old slipper, which is not only easy to carry but it also has the strong scent of you, the handler. Naturally, once the dog is holding something he classes it as his own, his prize. You however, are the pack leader and it will be instilled in him later that whatever he has is yours also, but this need not be put in too soon or else he will no doubt think, "If it is yours and all I do is fetch it for you, you get it yourself and you carry it!".

To start, offer the dog the slipper and when he takes it give *The Retrieve.* him plenty of fuss and praise, allow him to keep it, run around and play with it. If the dog returns to you, make another great fuss, give praise and allow him to continue. When the dog drops the article, recover it and take it away for another time. The article will become an even more prized possession if he realises that to drop it he will lose it.

Once the dog is readily holding the article, take him for a walk on the lead letting him carry it. Every now and then turn left, in front of the dog to stop and face him, put him in the sit position, wait a couple of seconds and then with a command of LEAVE take the article from him. Again wait a couple of seconds, give the article back, return to the heel side and continue the walk. After doing this two or three times, give plenty of praise when taking the article then put it away, out of sight.

If the dog is very possessive with the article and will not release it when commanded, a sharp tap on the rump, given by an accomplice at the same time as the command LEAVE is given, will provide the desired result. The dog must be facing you at this time and be unaware as to the source of the shock. If done correctly, the dog will think that your voice caused it and will therefore not risk disobeying in the future. If you force a dog to release his grip by taking hold of the muzzle you will, with the inevitable pressure used, possibly cause him to be hand-shy in this exercise.

Once the dog is proficient in carrying and giving up the article to hand, he can be taught the retrieve exercise. With the dog on a long lead, tease him with the article and then throw it a few feet. Immediately run with the dog, giving the command FETCH, and allow him to recover the article. Giving plenty of praise, jog backwards a short distance, reeling the dog towards you and coming to a stop, placing the dog in the sit position. Wait a few seconds before taking the article from him. If the dog is prone to dropping the article as you go to take it, the best method is to bring the hands up, from underneath the dog's chin, so if there is a drop it will not fall to the floor. The lead can be dispensed with once the dog is performing well and as this is achieved then so can the distance of the throw be increased.

Keeping the dog back for a few moments, after throwing, will increase his ability to use his nose and search. Eventually on hearing the command FETCH the dog, if seeing nothing thrown, will automatically put his nose to the ground and start searching. He will by this method recover anything with human scent on it, thus becoming ideal in the search for lost or hidden property.

The Sendaway

This exercise has no real purpose for the average pet owner other than to show control. It is, however, a pleasure to watch and is another method of 'running the dog'.

Control is paramount and should not be contemplated until the dog is proficient in the DOWN and will drop immediately. For the sendaway to be achieved, the dog must have the incentive to leave you, to go to something ahead, not merely leave your side. The finest sendaways to be seen are those of the sheepdog gathering his sheep, the sheep being the incentive to go out. Praise will not be an incentive, nor will it give the dog a direction, something has to be out there waiting and be visible. If there is nothing visible, but is out there, it will only teach the dog to wander and search. I prefer the incentive of food whereby the dog can be rewarded immediately but I will also explain how a ball can be used.

The equipment neeeded is a wooden stake and a traffic cone. Find a field free from any distractions, place the cone on the ground with the stake through the centre, thus not allowing it to be moved. With the dog on the lead, show the dog a biscuit, place it at the base of the cone and retreat a few yards backwards. Release the dog from the lead with a gentle command of AWAY, at which he will run to the biscuit and eat it (his reward!), then give the command of DOWN. Run to the dog, ensuring he remains down, give plenty of praise and repeat the exercise. The distance can be gradually increased. The dog, having the reward waiting, will perform it at speed.

One now asks, 'When do I stop having the dog on the lead and retreating from the cone?' When the dog is starting to become proficient, retreat from the cone but then instead of immediately releasing him hold back for a few minutes before sending him. This time lapse can be increased considerably until one takes the step of placing the cone/biscuit without the dog being present. Return with the dog to a point approximately 20 yards from the cone which should be clearly in view. Give the command AWAY, the dog should respond by running freely to the cone, finish the exercise as before. When the dog is eager and profficient then the discipline of a STAND or SIT can be introduced before the AWAY command. Next comes the question, 'When do I do away with the cone?' My answer is 'Never', always have the cone out there, but it can be out of sight at the beginning so that the dog has to go 50-100 yards before seeing it. I have never found any need to sit astride the dog to point it, or use any method other than him being at my side, the dog will take his direction from which ever way you are facing. If entering 'Working Trials', or simply on display, by the time the dog has run out a 100 yards, or more, you will have completed the exercise by putting him in the down position. It is advisable not to do a recall on this exercise, except when under test conditions, always join the dog.

The ball method is to place the ball under the cone, train the exercise as before, but now the dog has to wait for you to join him to retrieve and throw it.

Chapter 15

Novelty Tricks

Shaking Hands
With your dog in the sit position facing you, give the command SHAKE HANDS. Holding out your right hand tap him gently under his left foreleg until he raises his paw. Take hold of his paw with the right hand and give him a morsel of food with your left. Give a gentle shake of the paw before letting go, you are then ready to repeat the exercise.

Make A Bow
Having placed your dog in the stand position with the command STAND, with the hand under both forelegs, gently draw the legs forward, repeating the command MAKE A BOW, MAKE A BOW. If he starts to lie down, as he most probably will, raise his hindquarters from underneath, with your free hand. If the dog insists on trying to lie down then a block of wood or other object can be placed beneath him. Once the body position is reached, continue the same command, together with a gentle pressure on the top of the head until it rests on the paws. Keep in position for a couple of seconds and then finish the exercise, remembering to give plenty of fuss and praise.

Walking Through Your Legs
This exercise is more suitable for small dogs or people with long legs, as the dog is required to zig-zag through the legs of his walking handler. With the dog on the lead, at the heel side, take a large exaggerated step forward with the right leg. Pass the lead between the legs, pulling the dog through with the command WALK THROUGH. This is then repeated with the left leg, gradually speeding things up until there is no pause.

Rolling Over

This is quite an unnatural exercise for the dog and can be somewhat frightening to him at first try.

With collar and lead in place, the first part of the trick is to have your dog lying on his side. Then with your foot trapping the lead to the floor, a short distance from the collar, effectively controlling the dog, place one hand under the shoulder on which he is laying and with the other hand take hold of both forelegs. With a gentle pull of the legs and push of the shoulder turn the dog over, as in a 'roll', using the command ROLL OVER. Immediately the roll is complete, step off the lead, in order that the dog is free and don't spare the praise. This will require a lot of time and patience to succeed.

Chapter 16

COMMON BEHAVIOUR PROBLEMS

Jumping Up

The instinctive greeting by a dog is for it to jump up and endeavour to make the greeting face to face. This possibly stems from the wild state when it was natural for the puppy to greet returning adult dogs by licking around their mouths in the hope of a regurgitated meal. If you speak to the dog and lay hands on him, even in the act of pushing him away, it may be translated as a favourable response which will actively encourage the dog to do it again.

When your dog rushes to greet you, it must be a pleasurable experience for both parties concerned and to achieve this it must be controlled. First of all the dog must be actively discouraged from jumping up and this can be achieved by making the action uncomfortable. As the dog leaps a knee can be brought up to deflect him or both front feet taken hold of until the dog pulls them away. On both occasions, once the dog has all four feet back on the floor then bend or kneel down to his level and give plenty of praise.

If the dog is proficient at any of the control exercises, SIT, STAND or DOWN, then there should be no reason why the dog cannot be stopped in his tracks by using one of these. The praise then given can equally be for the greeting as well as completing the exercise. If food is used as an inducement, on each occasion, then you may find yourself involved in a high speed mugging.

Stealing

Dogs do not have the same moral values as us and they can never be classed as 'thieves', they are pure opportunists and if the occasion arises, they take it. What a wonderful world! There is no real cure, the best thing to do is to make sure that anything you do not wish the dog to have is out of his reach or by teaching the 'Retrieve' exercise, then anything he has will, on command, be brought back to you.

Chewing

All puppies chew, it is part of their learning experience. Whether by the feel or touch of things around them or breaking in new teeth, the need is there. Chewing itself is not so much a problem as 'what is being chewed'. You can teach what he is allowed to chew and what not to chew. The real problem is stopping chewing once it has started, for instance a kitchen unit, wallpaper or chair leg.

Praising the dog whilst he is chewing his play toy, rawhide or bone emphasises what he can chew but it does not cater for that 'one off' adventure. If the dog is caught chewing something he shouldn't then a verbal or physical reprimand can be given at that moment and the dog will realise he was doing something wrong. However if it is given sometime afterwards then he will not make that association. Once evidence is found that indiscriminate chewing has started then the object/s attacked must be protected from any further damage as well as remaining in position to allow correction to take place.

Any form of punishment technique by the owner, unless carried out expertly, will only succeed in preventing chewing in their presence. The idea is to get the dog to be the author of his own misfortune, a self-teaching exercise, in other words, to make indiscriminate chewing wholly disagreeable.

If the object being attacked is moveable then it can be 'booby trapped', taking care that this is done in such a manner as not to cause injury. A number of delicately placed tin trays, designed to fall the moment the object is touched will have a dramatic effect. Having the living daylights frightened out of him a couple of times should stop the habit forming. If the object is immovable and cannot be easily booby trapped then I have found a liberal sprinkling of cheap perfume on the object will also cause the chewing to cease. This has the effect of masking the personal dog odour left on it and also giving a foul prolonged taste.

A good large marrowbone is the normal answer to this problem.

Car Sickness

Car sickness occurs in dogs, just as in humans. Full-grown dogs that have never travelled in a car before can be prone to excessive drooling, sickness and in severe cases even defaecation. This is undoubtedly due to both physical and mental stresses.

A young puppy usually takes to car travel straight away without any problems at all, the whole world is new and a car is nothing exceptional. The mature dog is confronted with something that is large and noisy, claustrophobic, smelly and when it moves does all manner of things to the body, from being thrown around to stomach upheaval when going over humps.

Finding out a dog suffers from car sickness normally means that the poor dog has gone through torture before it is revealed, then it has a verbal earbashing before being thrown out while the mess is cleaned up, only to be put back in for the drive home, and the torture happens again . – with the same results! After his first car journey this dog has learned to fear the experience, which will only make matters worse for the next journey. This is the time to revert to square one.

Before even thinking of taking the dog for a ride, let it get used to the car. Allow the dog to spend some time in the car, without the engine running. Let it eat, sleep, do any manner of thing you will allow. Once the dog is used to that, then sit in the car with him with the engine running. When the dog is happy with that situation then take him for a 'short' ride, having made sure that he has had nothing to eat before. Ever increasing distances should provide the cure.

Barking In The Car
This problem has given me untold headaches, both from the actual barking and the mental anguish of trying to cure it.

The cause can be the same as car sickness and can be treated the same way. But if it continues and the dog is unresponsive to command i.e. the SPEAK exercise, I have yet to find a suitable method.

A water pistol has been suggested but I have found that although the bark does diminish it becomes a more nauseating whine, and the inside of the car gets wet through. (Trying to aim a water pistol at the dog's head in a moving car is quite some feat.)

A Few Don'ts

DON'T leave a dog in any vehicle without adequate ventilation especially on a hot summer day.

DON'T tie a dog to anything with a long line, it can easily become entangled causing strangulation.

DON'T throw any object which is hard and allow the dog to chase it whilst it is still in flight. The dog could catch it and break a tooth.

DON'T allow the dog to pick up stones, they cause the dog's teeth to wear down quickly and, of course, they can be swallowed.

DON'T leave a dog with any type of play toy which, if torn apart, can be swallowed and cause an obstruction. (I have known German Shepherd dogs brought into the kennels as 'gift dogs' and when examined, their insides have been found to contain plastic bags, socks, knickers etc.)

DON'T give the dog any heavy exercise after it has had a meal. It can not only cause the dog to vomit, but also cause a twisting of the stomach which inevitably results in death.

DON'T play tugging games. These are a test of strength and dominance and can easily, if involving a child, result in accidental injury either by the child being pulled over or bitten.

SNIPE TAFFY SWEEP BILL JERRY BEN

DON'T . . .
expect good
behaviour all the
time. Inspector
Joyce with
specialist search
dogs.

Part V

APPENDICES

Photograph courtesy of the Nottingham Evening Post.

In the whole history of the world there is but one thing that money cannot buy – to whit, the wag of a dogs' tail.

HENRY WHEELER SHAW (1818-85)

Dogs Within The Nottinghamshire Police Forces Before The Inception Of 'Dog Sections'

NOTTINGHAM CITY

Police Dog	Length of Service	Handler
BEN	1910 – 1914	(unknown)
DON	1911 – 1918	(unknown)
(unknown)	1911 – 1911	(unknown)
PRINCE	1912 – 1918	PC 308 Tuckwood
DUKE	1913 –	(unknown)
(unknown)	1914 –	(unknown)
(unknown)	1914 –	(unknown)
(unknown)	1918 – 1918	(unknown)
JACK	1918 – 1923	(unknown)

NOTTINGHAMSHIRE

Police Dog	Length of Service	Handler
DUKE (black labrador)	1938 – 1946	PC 111 Robinson

Nottingham City Police Dog Section (Formed 1954)
(* denotes a consecutive handler)

Police Dog	Length of Service	Handler
ROCKIE	1955 – 1966	PC 76 Walmsley
FRANKIE	1955 – 1959	*PC 430 Curtis *PC 701 Hall
STORM	1956 – 1958	PC 229 Knight
KIM	1956 – 1962	PC 336 Withers
KARL	1957 – 1958	PC 345 Hobson
DUKE	1957 – 1958	PC 702 Rollin
SILVER	1958 – 1959	PC 495 Joyce
PRINCE	1958 – 1963	PC 672 Westwood
DUKE II	1958 – 1962	PC 702 Rollin
BRUCE	1958 – 1965	*PC 458 Logan *PC 766 Carter
MAJOR	1959 – 1960	PC 731 Smith
RANGER	1959 – 1961	PC 701 Hall
JAKE	1959 – 1964	PC 328 Robinson
REX	1959 – 1961	PC 440 Murrin
KARL	1959 – 1970	PC 495 Joyce
JET	1960 – 1965	PC 450 Hayes
KING	1960 – 1968	PC 498 Pole
SILVER	1961 – 1964	PC 701 Hall
SILVER	1962 – 1972	PC 702 Rollin
SHANE	1962 – 1970	PC 726 Davies
SABRE	1963 – 1972	PC 672 Westwood
ROCKY	1963 – 1967	PC 518 Bennett
FRITZ	1964 – 1970	PC 147 Cooling

BLITZ	1965 – 1972	PC 541 Crosby
RUSTY	1965 – 1969	PC 450 Hayes
BRUTUS	1965 – 1970	PC 580 Johnson
CLINT	1965 – 1970	PC 766 Carter
JASON	1965 – 1972	PC 513 Cox
KIM	1966 – 1976	Sgt 64 Walmsley
BUSTER	1967 – 1974	PC 650 Simons
MAJOR	1967 – 1971	PC 752 Machin

Nottinghamshire Constabulary Police Dog Section (Formed 1956)

Police Dog	Length of Service	Handler
STARKE	1956 – 1963	PC 182 Sydenham
FREYA	1956 – 1959	PC 228 Johnson
HAGAN	1956 – 1967	PC 45 Lloyd
ARNO	1956 – 1965	PC 189 Smithurst
BRUCE	1957 – 1966	PC 184 Wood
RAS	1958 – 1962	PC 354 Harrison
REX	1959 – 1967	PC 323 Cuthbertson
SATON	1959 – 1968	PC 228 Johnson
WHISKY	1960 – 1963	PC 75 Brooks
BUTCH	1960 – 1966	PC 303 Scott
DANKO	1961 – 1961	PC 241 Clarke
WOTAN	1961 – 1968	*PC 182 Sydenham
		*PC 457 Cox
		*PC 260 Rebaudi
REX	1962 – 1972	*PC524 Ballington
		*PC 53 Wallace
KIM	1962 – 1973	PC 156 Houldsworth
BRUTUS	1963 – 1970	PC 58 Towlson
BARON	1963 – 1966	PC 575 Binch
MAJOR	1963 – 1966	PC 136 Wilson
SOLO	1964 – 1971	PC 585 Coulson
PRINCE	1964 – 1971	PC 96 Risely
SHADOW	1964 – 1972	PC 257 Dean
BRANDY	1964 – 1965	PC 421 Moeller
BLITZ	1964 – 1967	PC 45 Lloyd
CZAR	1964 – 1966	PC 41 George
RAYANT	1965 – 1968	PC 410 Ward
RUSTY	1965 – 1974	PC 399 Tindall
KING	1966 – 1970	PC 120 Fearn
WOLF	1966 – 1972	PC 136 Wilson
KIMBA	1966 – 1978	Sgt 184 Wood
BEN	1966 – 1970	PC 575 Binch
ROCKIE	1966 – 1966	PC 303 Scott

PRINZ	1967 – 1968	PC 410 Ward
QUELL	1967 – 1971	PC 311 Parkinson
INGON	1967 – 1973	PC 228 Johnson
IBEX	1967 – 1975	PC 137 Cook
PINZA	1967 – 1975	PC 323 Cuthbertson
REBEL	1967 – 1977	PC 45 Lloyd

Upon amalgamation of the two Police Forces, all County Officers added 800 to their existing shoulder number i.e. PC 666 Brown became PC 1466 Brown

Nottingham City Police Force and the Nottinghamshire Constabulary amalgamated in 1968 to form the Nottinghamshire Combined Constabulary to be later renamed in 1972 the

Nottinghamshire Constabulary Police Dog Section

Police Dog	Length of Service	Handler
OLAF	1968 – 1974	PC 665 Grocock
ETZEL	1968 – 1977	PC 498 Pole
CITO	1968 – 1972	*PC 993 Trolley
		*PC 1210 Ward
TAURUS	1968 – 1976	PC 477 Barnes
SIMBA	1969 – 1974	PC 1474 Fletcher
CHINDA	1969 – 1976	Insp Joyce
IKON	1970 – 1976	*PC 341 Tabernacle
		*PC 322 Curtis
CHASER	1970 – 1976	PC 1011 Parkinson
SABRE	1970 – 1979	*PC 614 Morley
		*Sgt 858 Towlson
SPARKY	1970 – 1976	PC 450 Hayes
BRIGAND	1970 – 1972	PC 361 Bricknall
JASON	1970 – 1978	PC 1476 Walton
KURT	1970 – 1977	PC 726 Davies
CHRISTIAN	1971 – 1982	PC 896 Risely
PRINTA	1971 – 1977	PC 626 Downing
BULLA	1971 – 1978	PC 797 Salmon
ROCKY	1971 – 1978	PC 1484 Duffy
ZAK	1971 – 1977	*PC 1011 Parkinson
		*PC 201 Murray
		*PC 1598 Kowalczuk
ALEX	1971 – 1973	PC 1508 Millington
SAM	1971 – 1975	PC 1385 Coulson
INCA	1971 – 1979	*PC 571 Kirkland
		*PC 1199 Tindall
JUNO	1971 – 1980	Sgt 841 George
CI	1971 – 1977	PC 541 Crosby
OSCAR	1972 – 1978	*PC 1573 Litchfield
		*PC 1508 Millington

BAT	1972 – 1977	PC 702 Rollin
KIEGER	1972 – 1974	PC 650 Simons
KABER	1972 – 1982	PC 936 Wilson
RINTY	1972 – 1979	*PC 1057 Dean
		*PC 541 Crosby
TEX	1972 – 1977	PC 853 Wallace
RORY	1973 – 1982	PC 1607 Fraser
FRAZER	1973 – 1978	PC 392 Harrison
GUS	1973 – 1974	PC 547 Harrison
NICK	1973 – 1977	PC 835 Tomlinson
CRAIG	1973 – 1981	PC 1482 Moore
BRETT	1973 – 1981	*PC 470 Cheetham
		*PC 1028 Johnson
		*PC 853 Wallace
ROYCE	1973 – 1980	PC 956 Houldsworth
BOSUN	1974 – 1978	*PC 665 Grocock
		*PC 147 Cooling
SCOTT	1974 – 1981	*PC 31 Davenport
		*PC 1834 Wharvell
RUDI	1974 – 1979	PC 1466 Brown
BLUE	1974 – 1982	PC 650 Simons
KELT	1974 – 1975	PC 547 Harrison
BRUNO	1975 – 1982	*PC 937 Cook
		*PC 498 Pole
FLAK	1975 – 1982	PC 1089 Hagen
SABA	1975 – 1977	PC 1687 Surgay
BRITT	1967 – 1982	*PC 616 Thornhill
		*PC 936 Wilson
SAXON	1976 – 1977	PC 1584 Lowe
JET	1976 – 1980	PC 1132 Bryan
ROSS	1976 – 1985	PC 450 Hayes
JED	1976 – 1986	Insp Joyce
KING	1977 – 1985	PC 241 Barnett
THOR	1977 – 1979	PC 1041 Keen
SOLOMON	1977 – 1981	PC 170 Vaughan
ROYAL	1977 – 1977	PC 1704 Kydd
ROB	1977 – 1983	PC 1627 Smith
SMOKEY	1977 – 1984	PC 1584 Lowe
FLINT	1978 – 1987	PC 240 Abbott
VADA	1978 – 1982	PC 1484 Duffy
DINO	1978 – 1986	PC 797 Salmon
MAC	1978 – 1984	PC 845 Lloyd
BRUTUS	1979 – 1985	PC 1741 Squires
CASS	1979 – 1983	Sgt 858 Towlson
ARRY	1979 – 1986	Ch/Insp Wood
KESS	1979 – 1986	Sgt 1199 Tindall
MURCO	1979 – 1986	*PC 898 Moore
		*Sgt 858 Towlson

BLITZ	1979 – 1988	*PC 1711 Curtis
		*PC 1117 Hill
SCHAEFER	1980 – 1985	PC 383 Wade
RYAN	1980 – 1986	PC 1466 Brown
KEY	1980 – 1983	PC 1132 Bryan
QUINN	1980 – 1986	PC 956 Houldsworth
SATAN	1980 – 1987	PC 1825 Kershaw
ARKO	1980 – 1985	PC 1041 Keen
MAX	1980 – 1988	Sgt 841 George
AXEL	1981 – 1984	PC 163 Cree
BEN	1981 – 986	PC 853 Wallace
SHANE	1981 – 1986	PC 1482 Moore
ZAK	1981 – 1983	PC 1834 Wharvell
CHARLIE	1981 – 1988	PC 1700 Vaughan
MOSTYN	1981 – 1983	PC 1797 Constantine
RIVA	1981 – 1988	PC 1843 Key
JAY	1982 – 1988	PC 1089 Hagen
REMY	1982 – 1985	PC 936 Wilson
DRIFTER	1982 – 1985	PC 479 Clifford
LUKE	1982 – 1987	PC 650 Simons
GRANITE	1982 – 1987	PC 498 Pole
JACK	1983 – 1985	PC 1797 Constantine
ROCKY	1983 – 1984	PC 1834 Wharvell
ZAK	1983 – 1986	PC 1132 Bryan
MITCH	1985 – 1993	PC1797 Constantine
KARL	1985 – 1991	*PC 163 Cree
		*Sgt 841 George
		*PC 1700 Vaughan
PADDY	1985 – 1988	PC 241 Barnett
KAISER	1985 – 1990	PC 1041 Keen
ERIK	1985 – 1992	PC 1834 Wharvell
ROMMEL/GREN	1985 – 1994	*PC 1584 Lowe
		*Insp Joyce
JASPER	1986 – 1988	PC 797 Salmon
ZEUS	1986 – 1993	PC 1741 Squires
SEBA	1986 – 1989	PC 383 Wade
RED	1986 – 1989	PC 1865 Adams
SAM	1978 – 1992	PC 59 Warner
ZAK	1986 – 1989	*Sgt 858 Towlson
		*PC 1843 Key
LASER	1986 – 1993	PC 1466 Brown
RODI	1986 – 1992	PC 1132 Bryan
SABRE	1986 – 1990	PC 853 Wallace
TROLL	1986 – 1987	PC 240 Abbott
ALEC	1987 – 1994	*PC 1825 Kershaw
		*PC 240 Abbott
JAKE	1987 – 1990	Sgt 108 Mellors

DIGGA	1987 –	PC 1933 Wilkinson
CAL	1987 – 1993	PC 1570 Walker
MATT	1988 – 1989	PC 1332 Croshaw
BOB	1988 – 1982	PC 1627 Smith
BRUNO	1988 –	PC 1117 Hill
SNAX	1988 –	PC 241 Barnett
LUKE	1989 – 1991	PC 805 McCarthy
BILL	1989 – 1994	*PC 1700 Vaughan
		*PC 853 Wallace
		*PC 1627 Smith
		*PC 1744 Chapman
BEN	1989 –	PC 1865 Adams
BLUE	1989 – 1993	PC 1843 Key
JACK	1989 –	PC 1332 Croshaw
KING	1989 –	PC 383 Wade
SWEEP	1989 –	PC 797 Salmon
BRENNON	1990 – 1994	*PC 554 Prince
		*Insp Joyce
REGAN	1990 –	PC 3 Raynor
BUSTER	1990 – 1993	*PC 1797 Constantine
		*PC 241 Barnett
VANCE	1990 – 1992	PC 1192 Savage
DEXTER	1990 – 1993	PC 174 Chapman
FRANKIE	1990 – 1993	PC 779 Partington
BO'SUN	1990 –	Sgt 973 Sanderson
KIP	1990 – 1994	PC 1041 Keen
REBEL	1990 –	Sgt 1474 Thompson
JIMMY	1990 – 1992	PC 1834 Wharvell
JOSS	1991 –	*PC 805 McCarthy
		*PC 45 Pepper
FRAZIER	1991 – 1992	PC 1973 Smith
SOV	1991 –	PC 1741 Squires
DREW	1991 –	PC 1480 Stirland
NICO	1991 –	PC 1700 Vaughan
QUINN	1992 –	PC 1132 Bryan
SOLOMON	1992 –	*PC 1627 Smith
		*PC 1741 Squires
SNIPE	1992 –	PC 1933 Wilkinson
ZAK	1992 –	PC 1865 Adams
DAN	1992 –	PC 1834 Wharvell
BAZ	1992 –	PC 59 Warner
TOM	1992 –	Sgt 1474 Thompson
WESSON	1992 –	PC 1973 Smith
THOMAS	1993 –	PC 1570 Walker
JERRY	1993 –	PC 1466 Brown
KELLY	1993 –	PC 779 Partington

BUSTER	1993 –	PC 1744	Chapman
BARNEY	1993 –	PC 1292	Pickersgill
KESTON	1993 –	PC 1797	Constantine
SAM	1993 –	PC 2037	Worrall
SABRE	1993 –	PC 449	Allsop
TAFFY	1993 – 1993	PC 241	Barnett
ZOLTAN	1993 –	PC 1070	Barker
RODDY	1993 –	PC 1402	Flint
JAKE	1993 –	PC 2002	Buckley
MIG	1993 –	PC 1843	Key
BEAU	1993 – 1994	PC 1173	Martin
DEX	1994 –	PC 240	Abbott
BUDDY	1994 –	PC 1834	Wharvell
WILF	1994 –	PC 1480	Stirland

Police Dog National Champions

Year	Dog	Handler/Force
1963	SKOL OF BASWICH	PC Smith (Staffordshire)
1964	SOMERPOL ZETA	PC Forsyth (Somerset)
1965	CHAN	PC Smith (Gloucestershire)
1966	GRIMPOL TEX	PC Raynor (Grimsby)
1967	SIMBA OF NORTHUMBRIA	PC Humphrey (Northumberland)
1968	Not contested	
1969	BRUCE	PC Colfer (Dorset)
1970	DIRK OF CADDUM	PC Scrimgeour (Glasgow)
1971	VICTOR OF AYCLIFFE	PC Dykes (Dundee)
1971	LANCON GUS	PC Nicholls (Lancashire)
1973	WESTYORKPOL KIMBA	PC Foster (West Yorkshire)
1974	QUIRK OF AYCLIFFE	PC Phillips (Hertfordshire)
1975	BOIS OF LIMBROOK	PC Lake (Metropolitan)
1976	LANCON SIMON	PC McNeille (Lancashire)
1977	NEYPOL KIMBA	PC Foster (North Yorkshire)
1978	ARNO	Sgt Scott (West Midlands)
1979	METPOL SABRE	PC Hosmer (Metropolitan)
1980	GLEN	PC Boyd (Royal Ulster)
1981	BONA	PC Clayton (North Yorkshire)
1982	ZIM	Sgt Womack (West Yorkshire)
1983	BONA	PC Clayton (North Yorkshire)
1984	SAXON	PC Fleet (Metropolitan)
1985	Not contested	
1986	INNSBROOK BENTYNE	Sgt Branley (Northumbria)
1987	SHANE	PC Rountree (Northumbria)
1988	CLEVEPOL KHAN	PC French (Cleveland)
1989	CLEVEPOL KHAN	PC French (Cleveland)
1990	BEN OF NEYPOL	PC Smith (North Yorkshire)
1991	OTTO	Sgt Walsh (Dorset)
1992	KESTON	PC West (Metropolitan)
1993	JACK	PC Griffiths (West Midlands)
1994	CHAD	PC Eaton (Northamptonshire)